DESTINATION
HAPPINESS

Everything you need to know to stay on course!

ALICE INOUE

All products available at Amazon.com, www.aliceinoue.com, and www.aliceinspired.com.

Printed by Createspace, an Amazon.com company.

Copyright © 2012 Alice Inoue Life Guidance, LLC

ISBN: 1479263427

ISBN 13: 9781479263424

Also by Alice Inoue

Books

A Loving Guide to These Shifting Times
Be Happy! It's Your Choice
Feng Shui Your Life!
Just Ask Alice!

DVDs

Feng Shui Demystified
Office Feng Shui
Feng Shui Illuminated – FAQs on Feng Shui

Unlike the goal of most journeys, getting to the end is not the goal of life.

.

Dedication

Dr. John Demartini

Your life's work has provided me with extraordinary wisdom and inspiration. Thank you for making an incredible difference in my life and in the lives of others.

Special Acknowledgment

Alan Wong

Day after day, month after month, year after year, you are there for me with your generous and indispensable guidance, wisdom, love, and support. I continue to be inspired by you every day. Thank you so much for all you do.

Acknowledgments

Sarah Aschenbach – I continue to thank my lucky stars that we found each other. Your editing of my work is always the best part about every book I write. I am looking forward to working with you on book six. You are truly amazing!

John De Mello, Kris Labang and Jayson Tanega – Thank you for your awesome photographic talents. The book cover came together for me perfectly because of you. I am forever thankful!

Erin Ushijima, Gay Dochin, Kay Yara, and Kimi Morton – Thank you for your insights, your time, and for reviewing the final manuscript for me. Most important, thank you for your friendship and support. You have a special place in my heart, and I have so much love for each of you!

Special Thanks

My Team: Judy Segawa, Marie-Jose Noyle, Erin Ushijima, Kelly Sugano, and Karen Murashige – I appreciate your help in my business, your support of my work, and everything you do for me in-between! I could not do what I do if it were not for you and the role each of you plays in my life. I love you all so much!

Clients, Friends, and Family – Thank you for being in my life. I do what I do because of you.

A Note To The Reader

Although I give a lot of advice throughout this book, please keep in mind that I am not certified as a doctor, psychologist, healer, grief counselor, financial planner, or wellness practitioner. While I do share with you information that I have learned from professionals in these fields, none of what I share should be misconstrued or substituted for professional advice. My intent is to give you a synthesis of my insights and experiences.

The real names of the people mentioned in this book have been changed or omitted for reasons of confidentiality. In some instances, I created different scenarios to further protect their identities. Any coinciding details or circumstantial similarity to you or someone you know is purely coincidental. In all cases, however, I've done my best to share examples that will enable you to see the essential elements of the concept I want to clarify through real-life examples.

I hope that what I have found to be most helpful in my life will also be helpful to you. Your happiness depends on you, and your life is what you choose to make of it.

Destination Happiness

The Concept Behind the Book

Once I decided to write another book on happiness, I needed to decide on its format before I could begin. At first, I considered making a collection of useful insights about ways to find happiness in life. As I envisioned the book in its finished form, I felt it lacked creativity and style, and I wasn't inspired to write it. I knew I needed to figure out how to make it fun to write and fun to read.

It came to me in a flash a few days later as I was driving in my car, looking for a speed limit sign: and I knew I had found my answer!

I found hundreds of safety tips from driving experts on www.smartmotorist. com. As I read over the collection, I saw that many of them were directly relevant to the bigger picture of the journey through life. Therefore, I have translated some of these into happiness tips and rules for the road of life. Every chapter title is an expert driving tip that points to how you can have happiness as your constant companion so that the journey itself can be as fulfilling as your destination.

Table of Contents

Introduction

The Road of Life

....

Unlike the goal of most journeys, getting to the end is not the goal of life.

....

Are you enjoying your life? Are you looking forward to the day you finally get what you want in terms of a relationship, health, financial status, and career? If so, you are not alone. Every day, someone tells me about something he or she feels is lacking in life. It is common to view this void as the reason for not living a full and happy life.

Many people spend a lot of time wishing that their lives were different. Maybe you do, too, in some way. Do you sometimes envision a future in which your dreams are fulfilled and you are satisfied, or do you look back at your past and regret the choices you made? Clients often say to me, "Alice, I understand about being thankful, and I *am* thankful for the many things I do have, but parts of my life drag me down. How can I be happy all the time?"

What Happiness Is

So, what *is* happiness? I think of happiness as a deep sense of satisfaction about all aspects of life, as knowing beyond a shadow of doubt that everything is perfect, no matter what is going on. I see happiness as a state of physical, emotional, mental, and spiritual well-being and balance. Happiness is knowing that you are in control of your life.

The foundation of happiness is not built upon something that happens to you, like winning the lottery or getting a raise. When your happiness depends on something external that is out of your control, you live on an emotional rollercoaster, careening back and forth between opposing spectrums of emotion. If you want to experience a deep sense of satisfaction and balance, you must cultivate happiness from the inside out.

Happiness Comes from Understanding Life

Happiness evolves from truly understanding life and why you are here and what life has to show you. When you understand that the Universe operates in every single moment of your life, when you understand that it is working with you to help you evolve, your perspective on life can change. When you have a balanced perspective, you feel satisfied, centered, and poised, all of which are important components of happiness. Happiness emerges once you stop expecting life to be something it is not and accept it for what it is.

Happiness that comes from within is sustainable. If you desire emotional stability and would like to live longer and feel better, understanding and cultivating happiness is one of the best things you can do for yourself.

The Journey of Life

Our journey of life starts on the day we take our first breath and lasts until we take our last breath and return to the world of spirit. Records show that 156,000 lives end every day, lives represented by only a dash on a cemetery headstone.

Unlike the goal of many things we do, getting to the end is not the goal of life's journey. The goal of life is to wake up to all that life has to offer and to appreciate and *love* each step along the way. The more you understand how best to navigate your personal journey, the more you can enjoy it.

Why Write about Happiness?

I write about happiness because I think it's something everyone wants. Surveys on what people want in life consistently show happiness at the top of the list. According to the Global Happiness Organization, a worldwide survey showed that happiness was rated as the most important thing in life.

All other answers—a good job, a loving relationship, better health, more money—are what people *think* will bring them more happiness. Yet, the reality is, nothing outside you can make you happy.

I also write about happiness because of my background. There was a time in my life when, had there been a contest, I would have entered myself into the category of Most Unhappy Person. I constantly wished for a different life. I remember many nights when I prayed that I could wake up as different person in a different life. I hated my name, my looks, and my life. My personal perspective (which was all that mattered, right?) was that everything in my life was "bad." In retrospect, of course, I see things differently; however, the extreme unhappiness I experienced in my earlier years is what prompted me to look for the way to live a happier life

Happiness as It Is Portrayed

Society and the media program us to think that happiness comes from what we have attained in the form of status, power, money, goods, or events. When I was in my teens, in fact, my father told me that if I wanted to be a happy adult, I had to get an education and find someone rich to marry. He said that if I married for love, I would starve to death

Happiness Is within Your Control

Life is all about the journey, and happiness can be your constant companion if you put forth conscious effort to change your old patterns. In this book, you will find some basic rules of the road that will keep you pointed in the right direction. The more you understand the journey of life and the bigger picture of how it all works, the easier it will be for you to reach "destination happiness."

Your perception of the world may be one that places happiness out of your control when, in fact, it is completely within your control no matter what your circumstances. I am committed to embracing ever-higher levels of happiness as I journey through life. I plan to leave the planet smiling, with the dash on my headstone curved up into a smile.

ONE

DRIVE LIKE YOU OWN THE CAR, NOT THE ROAD

You only have control over yourself.

You own your car, but you do not own the road, although many people drive as if they do. You can tailgate to pressure other drivers to move faster, you can lean on your horn, you can drive maddeningly slow in a no-passing lane just to prove a point, you can make unexpected moves that endanger your life and everyone else's—but you still can't control the other drivers unless they let you. Ultimately, you are only making yourself more impatient and unhappy by trying to exert control over others. As a driver, your goal must be to take responsibility for your destination, maintain control of your car, follow the rules of the road, and enjoy the ride.

Similarly, you own your life. You are the only one who experiences it, and the truth is, you are the only one you can trust to be with you for the rest of your life. People and experiences continually come and go, and all of it will add to your journey. However, your life is for *you* and no one else, and this is why it's important to understand how to take charge of it.

There is no one on earth or in the heavens above who can give you happiness or take away your pain. No one can live your life for you. You are in full control, whether you think so or not, and if you are not happy with your life today, chances are you won't be happy with your life tomorrow, either, unless you decide to make some changes.

Life Is Challenging

Is your life a constant challenge? Many people tell me that their life is more challenging than most. Madelyn immediately comes to mind when I think of someone who is unhappy with her life. She came to see me because she was at her wits' end. She felt that no one respected her and that everyone, from her husband to her kids to her boss, drained her energy with their demands. She felt guilty and selfish if she said No, so she did it all, plus more. As a result, she had no time for herself and felt that no one cared about her happiness or what she wanted in life. She also hated her job, her demanding boss, and felt uninspired most of the time. The bottom line was that she felt she had lost control of her life somewhere along the way and didn't know how to get it back.

How can Madelyn ever be happy? What does she have to change about her life? Does she need to learn how to say No? Should she have a retreat at the spa once a month? Should she take some time to meditate and center each morning? Or does she need to look at her life in a different way? She definitely has a lot of options to choose from if she wants to take action, but for her to get to a better place sooner rather than later, she would first need to start seeing her life in a very different way.

You Are In the Driver's Seat

No matter what the challenge, the first and most important step to take on the path toward happiness is to see that you *are* in the driver's seat of your life no matter what is going on; you are in full control, as unlikely as that may seem at first.

If you think about it, every single situation you are in, whether you think of it as good or bad, is in your life because of choices you make about how you see it and how you react to it. Sometimes, we feel like a victim of circumstances, but we never are. We have the power within us to see that we are in control.

You may be thinking of scenarios like robbery, rape, unplanned pregnancy, and betrayal. These are events that no one "chooses" to have happen, and you may wonder how these are choices people make. Of course, no one consciously chooses such challenges, and though they come into our lives for reasons we may not understand from our current level of consciousness, we do have the power in each moment to make choices about how an event affects us and our quality of life.

What Are You Choosing to Focus On?

The factor that defines your experience of past or present events and situations is what you focus on. Do you hold on to anger, blame, and judgment? Do you choose to use what happened as an excuse for why you are not where you want to be in life? You are in full control of how you choose to process everything that is going on in your life every day.

It is vital to let go of the "I-can't-help-how-I-feel" mindset and affirm that you *can* help how you feel if you take a long look at your perspective on events in your life that you perceive are "causing" your unhappiness and your judgments about them. This book will show you ways to do this, but the first step is to recognize that you do have the control.

In Madelyn's case, I started by helping her see that she was more in control than she realized—that she actually was *choosing* to do what she was doing, even though she felt that those choices were being forced upon her. In reality, she was making choices that gave her the best advantage. Other choices would have caused her more unhappiness. If she said No to everyone, not only would she feel guilty, but she also would judge herself for being selfish and beat herself up internally for being a bad mother and wife. The people around her would give her grief for not doing what they expected of her, and then she would feel worse—isolated and alone. As well, if she quit her job, not only would she feel like a failure, but also having no income would be more stressful than staying in a job she didn't like.

Although Madelyn felt drained, resentful, and unhappy and thought she was "out of control," she actually was quite "in control," that is, she was making the best choices each day to minimize her challenges given the set of circumstances she was in and the beliefs she had formed about her life. Even though she didn't like the reality of her situation, once she recognized that she was in control, we began creating opportunities for her to change her perceptions so that she could make different choices.

Every Day, Affirm That You Are in Control

The understanding that you are in control has to be the foundation upon which you base your life, even if you feel everything is out of your control. Affirm this phrase to yourself daily: "I am in control of every aspect of my life and am responsible for everything I experience, whether I like it or not, whether I understand it or not, or whether I want it or not." Knowing that you are in control of your life is the first step.

Say Goodbye to Blame

Once you recognize that you are in control of your life, ask yourself whether you consciously or subconsciously blame others for your challenges. Blame is the one thing that renders us powerless and takes us away from being in true control of our lives. It can be difficult, if not nearly impossible, to understand how the predicament you are in is anything but the fault of others. However, no matter the situation or who you think is wrong, it is beneficial to adopt the mindset that nothing happens *to* you and that everything happens *for* you. As the Dalai Lama says, "If you choose to blame, only you will suffer."

It is understandable that Madelyn blamed everyone around her for her life and complained that no one cared that she was tired and unhappy. She felt that everyone was selfish and insensitive and that this was the reason she was trapped in her life. "Can't they see what they are doing to me?" she lamented. "If only my husband would be less demanding, my kids more appreciative, and my co-workers less negative, I would feel better and have more time for myself. I would be so much happier." She was waiting for them to wake up to what was going on with her.

I explained that everything this collective situation was doing *to* her that she hated was actually, in the grander scheme of things, being done *for* her so that she could become empowered and see the situation from a different perspective. Until she could take responsibility and look at her life 100 percent in terms of herself, she would forever feel that others were to blame in part or in whole for where she was at in her life.

Three Questions

I asked Madelyn three questions that I recommend you ask yourself:

Are you open to looking for a new perspective?

- Do you think it is possible to feel better about your life?
- Are you willing to redirect blame and take responsibility in a new way?

Unless you can answer Yes to all three, you won't get very far on the journey towards happiness and self-empowerment.

After we had worked together for a while, Madelyn eventually broke down and realized that it wasn't everyone else who needed to make changes; it was her. Once she redirected her blame, took responsibility, and opened up to changing her perspective, Madelyn felt hopeful that she could feel better. As a result, her feelings about her life changed significantly, even though no one around her had changed.

Old Perceptions Are Hard to Break

Old perceptions are hard to break; it seems so much easier to live in blame, expecting everyone else to change. However, if you want to step up to a new level in life, you have to get over the resistance—not just your resistance to some things, but your resistance to *everything* in your life.

It is helpful to ask yourself how you are benefiting from a challenging situation. Clients often tell me they can't understand how there can be a benefit to what they are going through. How can losing a large sum of money, getting sued, suffering a betrayal, or getting hit by a drunk driver *benefit* them? The benefits are always there, but when we focus on the challenges and the unfairness of it all, we remain blind to any benefits we are receiving. Looking for the benefits is how you begin the process of shifting your perspective about a situation.

When I asked Madelyn what benefits she got from the challenges, she kept saying, "None." She had gotten so caught up in being stuck in her life that she couldn't even see one benefit to her life as it was. I knew that she had to be getting something out of her life, so I gave her an assignment: Find the benefits of doing what you are doing.

Possible Benefits of Doing What You're Doing

Madelyn came back with a long list of benefits that she uncovered after a lot of thinking and inner searching. Some of these were:

- She felt proud that she could juggle and do so much.
- She liked feeling that her family depended on her.
- She felt safe and comfortable playing her role.
- She felt indispensable when her family needed her.
- She liked it when others told her she was a good mother and good wife.
- She could use her family as an excuse to decline unwelcome invitations.
- She could use her unhappiness as something to complain about.
- She didn't have to learn anything new.
- She had an excuse for why she wasn't "further along" in her life.
- She could use her tiredness as an excuse not to be intimate with her husband.
- Her challenging boss gave her something to complain about with her friends.

You can use the benefits that Madelyn found to stimulate your own thinking. What are the benefits you gain from doing what you are doing?

A New Perspective Does Wonders

Once you commit to a practice of looking for and finding the benefits of your challenges, they will cease to push your buttons and drain your energy in the way they do now, putting you back in control.

Although you still may not like what is going on, you will be able to see it in a new light; as a result, you can't help but feel better about it. Remember, the world is conspiring to help you at all times, whether you see the benefit in the moment or not, and the challenges in your life are one of the ways it does this. You are not here on earth to have an easy life. You are here on earth to experience all facets of life, to understand the divine order that exists, and to feel the ever-present love.

Madelyn's Progress

Although she still dreamed of the day when everyone would appreciate her and still had trouble saying No to old habits, Madelyn realized that she had to keep working on herself. She no longer had a fantasy about how life *should* be, and she no longer hated her life to the same degree. Six months later, she is not even close to where she ultimately wants to be; however, she feels confident that she is moving towards what she wants every day because she knows that she is in charge. She openly admits that she was waiting for everyone else to save her when what she really needed was to save herself. The best part is that she has taken back the reins of her life.

Look for the Bigger Picture

We often hate our biggest challenges as we are going through the emotional chaos and mental stress. We complain, get angry, plot revenge, and wait for the day the challenge will pass only to look back a little further down the road and say, "I'm so glad that happened. Look where I am today because of that." I'm sure we've all experienced something we considered our biggest challenge turn out to be our biggest blessing. And we've all had situations we thought were blessings that turned out to be our biggest nightmares.

When we were going through the emotionally challenging times, if we had looked for the bigger picture of how we were gaining, we would have seen more of the benefits of what was going on and perhaps would have saved ourselves some unnecessary sadness. No matter what is going on, the way to get present with your life is to trust that there is a divine order and a hidden balance and recognize that it is up to you to look for them. There is a reason for everything that happens, and there is no one to blame for anything, not even yourself. There are hidden benefits to all challenges, and hidden challenges to all benefits. All challenges lead us to grow by providing lessons we would not have chosen otherwise.

Repeating Challenges

What about the challenges that come back just when we thought we had gotten rid of them? When we repeatedly get caught up in the same type of challenging situation, it is because we are not getting the lesson that life is trying to teach us. As you may have noticed, women or men who have low self-esteem often attract partners who put them down. When one relationship ends, they walk right into another one that has the same abusive dynamic. You may know someone who says, "Why do I keep attracting the wrong type of guy?" The reality is that she is attracting exactly the right type of guy, one who gives her ample opportunity to see her value and raise her self-esteem. Once she "gets it," she not only will get out of the relationship, she will stop attracting "that" type of guy. All her abusive relationships are helping her get the message that she has a value she has not been honoring.

Arina is an accountant with her own business. Clients took to her right away and trusted her because of her engaging personality. She prided herself on the quality of her services, but for some reason, she kept attracting clients who, according to her, "are nice at first and then become demanding jerks who criticize the quality of my work." Finally, two clients threatened to file lawsuits because of something they felt she should have done and didn't.

She couldn't understand why this was happening to her, and she was angry and hurt. She worked with me on and off, and whenever we got to the part where I said that there was a message for her and suggested she look deeper, she disappeared. She couldn't accept what I was saying and get past her self-righteousness and her certainty that she was right and they were wrong. Interestingly, I ran into her the other day. She is still telling the same story, and challenging clients continue to be attracted to her.

I know that until Arina gets the message and develops the awareness to look inside and see that her "I-am-better-and-I-am-right" attitude is drawing challenging clients to humble her, she will continue to live the same story.

Wishing for Your Life to Change Is Wasted Energy

Even though you may want only "good" things to happen to you, if that really were the case, you would be lazy and uninspired. You wouldn't grow, and life would be meaningless. If you see your challenges only as drawbacks and fail to look for the benefits they present, life feels too tough, and you burn out.

Wishing your life would change is wasted energy. The most effective approach is to open up to reality and expect that your life will bring people, situations, and circumstances that are both challenging and supportive. By doing so, you will engage with life more fully and, as a result, will be in the best position to navigate whatever comes your way.

Key Points

- You own your life and are the only one you can trust to stay with you for the rest of your life.
- You are in full control of your life, and you are making all the choices.
- Knowing you are in control of your life is the first step. Affirm: "I am in control of every aspect of my life and am responsible for everything I experience and everything I feel, whether I like it or not, whether I understand it or not, or whether I want it or not."
- If you want to move forward in life, you must be able to answer Yes to these three questions:

  ✓ Are you open to a new perspective?
  ✓ Do you think it's possible to feel better about your life?
  ✓ Are you willing to redirect blame and take responsibility?

- Take responsibility for yourself.
- Remember that nothing happens *to* you, and everything happens *for* you.
- Find the hidden benefits of your challenges to gain a new perspective.
- Look back to see how challenges in the past have led to where you are today.
- If you have repeating challenges, find the lesson, get it, and move on.
- The reality of life is that we will never get away from the polarity, so embrace both sides for empowerment.

TWO

PREPARE FOR UNEXPECTED EVENTS

Surprises in life steer you in new directions.

One day not long ago, I ran from my office to my car so I could drive to a big wedding I was officiating. I was running a little late, so of course I was hoping that I would not run into any afternoon traffic. When I saw my car, it turned out that traffic was the least of my worries. I had a flat tire! "Of all times, why *now?*" I sighed.

At that moment, the security guard magically appeared and offered to help me put my spare tire on. I exhaled, gratefully accepted, and figured that if we could change it quickly, I would be able to start the wedding on time. We opened the trunk only to find that my spare tire was flat. I called a taxi that came right away, fortunately, and I made the wedding on time. It was a close call and I was relieved.

However, when I arrived at the hotel for the formal, upscale wedding, I realized that, in my haste, I had left the white shoes that match my white robe in my trunk. I knew I couldn't perform the ceremony with the casual slippers I had on, so I talked a hotel employee who was walking by into letting me borrow her formal shoes for twenty minutes. (Yes, I was desperate.) Although they were the wrong color and three sizes too big, I was thankful to have shoes and to make it to the ceremony on time.

Later, I pondered the event. Why did I have to get a flat tire then? Why couldn't it have been on my way home after the wedding? I knew there had to be a reason.

Sure enough, on the taxi ride home, inspiration struck. I had been wondering what hotel catering offices and wedding coordinators did if a minister didn't show up due to an emergency. What if I had been on the other side of the island and unable to get a taxi so quickly? A wedding ceremony can begin without the musicians or the flowers, but not without the minister. This train of thought gave me the idea to offer officiant training classes to those in the wedding business, enabling them to assure their wedding clients that, no matter what, they would have a licensed officiant on site to marry them. I probably would never have thought of this possibility had I not had that flat tire. Because of my close call, many wedding business owners in Hawaii are now licensed as officiants.

Synchronicity

Everything that happens in our lives happens for a reason, even if at the time we don't understand what that reason is. There is always a bigger picture, an underlying pattern, and overlying order to our seemingly random life events. In every moment, situations, circumstances, thoughts, emotions, actions, relationships, and people all interact in perfect synchronicity as life moves forward. Through the lens of our awareness and our level of consciousness, we judge these synchronicities to be good, bad, or neutral.

However, no matter what, synchronicities of all types show up in our lives to point us toward a new direction of thought, action, or awareness. The key is to remain open to life in all its unexpected manifestations, so that occurrences that are outside of our control do not end up taking control of our lives.

Don't Be Too Quick to Judge Unexpected Events

As a child, I heard a story that illustrates why we should not judge unexpected events as either good or bad, but rather keep a neutral perspective, a wait-and-see attitude.

A Chinese farmer in a small village had one horse, and it ran away. Since the village was so poor, his friends and neighbors came by to sympathize: "It is horrible and unfortunate that your horse has run away!" The farmer replied, "Maybe."

The next day, the horse came home, bringing with him many wild horses. "Wow, how fortunate!" said the friends and neighbors. "Maybe," replied the farmer.

When the farmer's son was trying to tame one of the wild horses, he was bucked off and broke his leg. "How awful!" said the friends and neighbors. "Maybe," said the farmer.

Later, an army passed through the village, recruiting all able-bodied young men. The farmer's son was passed over because of his broken leg. "How lucky you are," the friends and neighbors said.

How do you think the farmer replied?

This story demonstrates how, too often, we judge events from a limited perspective. Sometimes, what initially looks desirable can turn out to be undesirable, or what initially looks undesirable can turn out to be desirable.

Synchronistic Events

To expand this concept further, imagine that you are in an elevator. The doors open, and in steps a long-lost childhood friend that you have been looking for but have had no luck finding. You would be overjoyed at this amazing synchronicity and think, "Wow! What are the chances? This is wonderful!"

On the other hand, if the person who enters the elevator is the man you recognize as the driver who put your mom in a wheelchair for months, you would be distressed and think, "Oh, my God! Get me out of here. This is horrible. What did I do to deserve this?"

What could be the purpose of two such unexpected encounters? Following the example, we would naturally see the friend encounter as the "good" one and the driver encounter as the "bad" one. From a universal viewpoint, however, both events would be neutral and showing up in your life simply to point you toward a new direction of thought, action, or awareness.

Enter the Unexpected

Imagine the first scenario carried a few months into the future. You and your childhood friend are now in touch regularly. You jumped back into the relationship with open arms and without knowing that she is emotionally needy. She takes up a lot of your time and depends on you to cheer her up. The "divine synchronicity" you initially thought was so good turned out to be not so good. However, having your old friend come into your life is helping you redefine your values and learn to draw your boundaries in a new way. You might recognize that your synchronistic meeting was part of a bigger picture that was initially hidden.

Let's move on to the second scenario. Imagine that the thirty seconds you spent in the elevator with the driver who injured your mom forced you to reflect on the events of the past and prompted a moment of awareness. Let's say that you and your mother, who had had an oppositional relationship in the past, were given an opportunity to unite on the same side because of the accident, which as a result brought you closer. Now your relationship with your mother has reached a whole new level. You might then see that the accident was a gift. The bigger picture involved in encountering the driver who caused the accident was the opportunity it gave you to appreciate the benefits as well as to bring closure to the past.

The bottom line is this: No matter what happens in your life, whether it is expected or unexpected, desirable or undesirable, and whether you judge it as good or bad, is there to serve you in unimaginable ways. The key is to affirm that all events are neutral and not be attached to the outcome.

Life Is Full of Surprises

We don't like chaos or unexpected challenges, so we may spend a lot of energy planning, predicting, and resisting events that can't be planned, predicted, or prevented, even with the best of life planning skills. When we are attached to a specific outcome, it is hard not to feel angry, frustrated, or let down when things turn out differently, even if at some level we know that what happened will lead us to a better place, eventually.

It is important to remind yourself often that much of the beauty in life comes from the way it surprises you. Life renews itself constantly, and usually these very surprises bring new direction. The unexpected events that surprise us often bring us things we don't even know we are looking for. Even so, initially the unexpected can be stressful.

How to Navigate Unexpected Events

Accepting the fact that we live in a world that is guaranteed to surprise us with unpredictable occurrences and allowing things to unfold without overstressing yourself is a skill that you can practice and improve on. It takes conscious awareness and effort to learn new skills that will help you respond to life's spontaneity with greater ease, but it is worth it.

When the unexpected throws you off course, follow these steps:

1. **Remind yourself that you can't control everything.** We all know this at some level, yet often the way we act and feel is contrary to this basic truth. When something happens that is outside of your control, take a deep breath and remind yourself that the unexpected is a normal part of life. By doing so, you record a different response in your physiology and in your memory.

2. **Don't dwell on why it happened to you.** You can find the greater meaning, later. It is more important to ask yourself what you can do immediately to meet this challenge in a way that will bring about the best possible outcome. Instead of putting your focus on what went wrong, step out of the chaos right away. Don't waste any time wishing it didn't happen.

3. **Stop for a moment and take a break.** If the momentum of the event is forcing you to make a decision right away, at least make sure you take a break first. If you are in your office, take a walk. If you are in a meeting or at home, use the restroom. Detach from the chaos, move to a different physical area, take a deep breath, and remind yourself of Number 1 and Number 2 above.

4. **Remember that what you are feeling and experiencing is temporary.** Sometimes, in the midst of a storm, we see no end in sight. Remind yourself that every situation has a conclusion. Even if the conclusion turns out to be what you didn't want, remember that there is a bigger picture at play and trust that. If something has to be redone, you will likely end up doing it better.

5. **Ask for help.** When we are thrown off balance, the mind usually takes over, and we start managing everything in our heads. Fear can easily show up and throw us into a state of overwhelm. Talk to someone who is detached from the situation and can help you see what's going on from a different perspective. Choose someone who is calm and heart-centered. Another person may be able to offer you useful insight that will help bring you back to your own heart center, where you can recognize that the situation has come up as part of a greater purpose.

6. **Don't take it personally.** Although it may feel like the universe and others are conspiring against you, especially when everything seems to go wrong all at once, know that what is happening is just part of the path of life and you will move through it. Don't jump to conclusions, and remember that no matter how you view the situation, there are other sides of the story to consider.

7. **Remember that you can't control others**. If the situation has arisen because someone else didn't follow your advice, that is frustrating, to say the least, especially when it is someone you are close to. Reaffirm to

yourself that the other person is simply doing what he or she feels is most important, even if you disagree. As I mentioned in Number 6, do not take it personally.

8. **Redirect blame, look for the benefit, and view the situation from a new perspective.** Turn the attention back to yourself and use the information I shared in Chapter One. It will help you find the value in what life is bringing you so that you can come to a more balanced perspective. Remember, this is not happening *to* you; it's happening *for* you. Where might the value be, given what has happened? How can you benefit?

9. **Envision the outcome you desire.** Think about the outcome you want, given your current situation, the new information you have at hand, and the resources available to you. Lay out your options, make a decision, and commit.

10. **Move forward.** Even if your options are limited, even if the situation is not what you originally hoped for, accept that it is the best it can be under the circumstances and move forward, trusting that there is a bigger picture and that you will come out better for this experience.

Expect the Unexpected

The unexpected will happen. The best you can do is be ready to deal with it when it does. Preparing for the unexpected does not mean you are inviting challenges into your life; rather, preparation shows that you understand the duality of life is real and that you are equipped to navigate the turbulence smoothly.

The Big Challenges

There is not much you can do to prepare yourself for life-altering events, such as an unexpected death in the family, a sudden illness, losing all your possessions in a fire, getting fired, or navigating a divorce, to name a few. The one thing you can do is to remember: "This too shall pass." As hard as it seems in the moment, life does go on. You can only do your best and focus on the support you have around you. Remind yourself that better times will come.

Working with people as an astrologer, I have seen many long-time clients go through the worst of times only to come out the other end and into new and wondrous beginnings. Ups and downs are part of the natural cycle of life. When you are up, look for the drawbacks. When you are down, look for the benefits. If you or someone you know is experiencing a challenging time, just take it day by day and prepare for better times ahead.

Be Realistic

Don't delude yourself into thinking that everything will go smoothly just because you have committed to make a change.

If you are planning to leave your job so you can look for a new job, be realistic in your planning and expect that things you don't expect may come up. Your co-workers may give you a hard time, you may have unexpected expenses, or something else may come up to keep you from quitting at the time you planned.

If you are eating a healthier diet, exercising, and losing weight, expect that sooner or later you will hit a plateau, get too busy to exercise or eat in the way you want to, fall victim to peer pressure, or get bored with the same old routine.

If you are in a new relationship, you may have disagreements, discover differences, and go through times where one of you wants to be alone more than the other. You may have to face money issues or work on other issues that come up.

Being Realistic Is Not the Same as Negative Thinking

Some people worry that thinking of all the "bad" things that can happen puts the focus on what you don't want and increases the chances that the "negatives" will come to pass. The reality is that being open to both the "positive" and the "negative" is a practice in balanced thinking. Balance is vital. If your head is flying in the clouds of fantasy or buried in the sands of resistance, you are closed to how life actually operates.

Accepting the possibility that something challenging *may* happen allows you to experience the natural ebb and flow of life and not get overly attached to an outcome. When you adopt a balanced mindset, your world won't come crashing down if something unexpected happens.

Everything Is Perfect Exactly as It Is

I often hear people say, "Nothing's perfect" when describing a situation that is not going according to plan. Nowadays, I say instead, "Everything is perfect," because as much as I may not like what has come up, I know and trust that there is a bigger picture.

Everything happens in our lives to serve a greater purpose for us and for the other people involved. There are always hidden benefits to our challenges and hidden challenges to our benefits. By keeping this in mind, we can move out of chaos and fear and into the knowing that everything will unfold exactly the way it needs to. Everything really is perfect.

Key Points

- Everything in life happens for a reason, even if you don't know what that reason is.
- Synchronicities point you toward new directions of thought, action, and/or awareness.
- From a larger perspective, all events are neutral, so refrain from judging them as good or bad.
- Everything that happens in your life happens to serve you in unimaginable ways, even if the events are stressful and unpleasant at the time.
- Ten ways to navigate unexpected events:

  - ✓ Realize you can't control everything.
  - ✓ Don't ask, "Why me?"
  - ✓ Stop for a moment and take a breather.
  - ✓ Remember that what you are feeling and experiencing is temporary.
  - ✓ Ask for help.
  - ✓ Don't take it personally.
  - ✓ Remember that you can't control others.
  - ✓ Redirect blame, look for the benefit, and view the event from a new perspective.
  - ✓ Envision the new outcome you desire.
  - ✓ Move forward.

- Expect the unexpected and prepare for it.
- In the case of a life-altering event, remember, "This too shall pass."
- When you are committing to something new, be realistic. Expect the unexpected.
- Everything is perfect, no matter how it feels. Trust that there is a bigger picture and a greater purpose for everything that transpires.

THREE

PACK ONLY WHAT YOU NEED

Leave hoarding and scarcity thinking behind.

You can choose one of two ways to pack for a journey: you can cram in everything that will fit "just in case," or you can pack only what you need, knowing that along the way you can find anything critical you have forgotten. When you cram in everything, your car is a mess and just finding what you packed can be a challenge.

Similarly, you can choose one of two ways to go through your life: you can collect and keep everything in sight just in case you may need it one day, or you can trust that everything will come to you exactly when you need it. Which one do you think allows you the most freedom and ease?

At first, it may seem that keeping everything is the best option, but actually, hoarding reflects a scarcity mindset, which is limiting and fear-based. Trusting that you will have what you need may seem risky, yet it is congruent with the nature of the universe we live in, and so it is actually the better choice. When you trust that everything will come to you when you need it, you will always receive exactly what you need in any given moment.

A Business Strategy Is a Life Strategy

After World War II, the executives at Toyota Motor Company in Japan decided to produce their cars in a new way. Instead of buying and storing massive stockpiles of supplies as other car manufacturers of that time did, they implemented a strategy of ordering their parts just before those parts were needed. Toyota's production dramatically increased and their profits went up. The new business practice became legendary because it was innovative. What Toyota pioneered came to be called just-in-time manufacturing, and it moved the entire industry away from a just-in-case inventory business practice.

Relating this business concept to scarcity thinking and abundance thinking brings valuable insight. If you feel overwhelmed, overburdened, and not as productive as you could be, you may be operating with a "just-in-case" mindset and would benefit by changing it to a "just-in-time" mindset.

Scarcity Thinking: Everything Good Is in Scarce Supply

There was a time in history when necessities were scarce for many. In some places of the world, this is still true, however most of us live in places where our basic needs are met. We have food, shelter, and clothing, yet we operate as though necessities are still scarce and good things are in short supply, which leads us to accumulate excess. Driven by an unconscious belief of lack, we accumulate more and more.

As a feng shui consultant, I often see homes that have too many things in them. This excess creates clutter and a stagnant atmosphere in the home. People who live in cluttered homes commonly share the same symptoms: they complain of overwhelm and laziness and say they procrastinate. Their lives match their environment.

Just-in-Case Excess in Other Areas of Life

Experts usually link scarcity thinking to excess clutter in the environment. However, I've noticed that areas of life other than the physical environment also are affected by scarcity thinking. I have seen scarcity thinking result in excess weight, excess insecurity in relationships, and excess anxiety over money.

Your home may be clutter-free, but do you suffer from excess in other areas of your life? Do you work too much, eat too much, buy too much, or cram too much into your schedule? Such actions may be fueled by a scarcity mindset.

Stubborn Pounds

It is now common knowledge that if you go on a diet that extremely limits calorie intake and starves your body, you will not be able to successfully control your weight long term. Starving activates the just-in-case mechanisms in your body to hold on to fat "just in case" you need it for the next famine. This is the same principle that links scarcity thinking to accumulating excess clutter.

However, what about people who are not starving their bodies or overeating yet still are holding on to excess weight? Wellness practitioners say that it can be emotional, that the excess weight serves as a buffer to insulate them from whatever they are not ready to face. According to this theory, people may say they want to lose weight but unconsciously they are not ready, so they keep the weight on without understanding why.

Another possibility to explain excess weight is scarcity thinking. A just-in-case mindset (fear) sends the body constant signals to hold on to excess weight—just in case. I have seen weight loss directly correlate to a shift away from scarcity thinking. The more secure and abundant people feel about themselves and their lives, the easier it is to let go of unwanted thoughts, emotions, and even excess weight.

Relationship Woes

Scarcity thinking when it comes to relationships can create challenges, as well. Some people, although they may not hoard objects and create clutter, instead may have a need to control other people by keeping a tight rein on them—just in case. When they believe that love is scarce, they cling to others and become demanding. When they perceive that love is missing, they try to hoard it and act in ways that make people want to run from them.

Money, Money, and More Money

I'm sure we all know people who have a healthy financial picture, yet still feel scarcity, anxiety, and hold on to just-in-case thinking. I have many clients who have enough money to last them literally the rest of their lives, yet their scarcity mindset will not allow them to enjoy life and use their money to help them achieve their goals. If the stock market takes a dip, they dip along with it, suffering from deep anxiety because their emotions and well-being are tied to their financial picture.

Voids Drive Us

Scarcity thinking is caused by fear of a void. When we feel a void or fear a void, we try to avoid it. For example, people who are deeply afraid of being alone will constantly surround themselves with people so they don't have to face it.

Of course, not all voids are "bad" and result in unwanted excess, as in the case of excess body weight. Our voids drive us and lead us to value what we feel we are missing. For example, my father never made it past the sixth grade, and my mother never went to high school, so they had a void when it came to education. So, guess what? Not surprisingly, my parents placed a high value on school and would go without in other areas so that I could have the best education they could afford.

When I was five years old, they entered me into first grade because I was "smart enough," yet because I was so much younger, I never got very good grades. Had I been in a class with others my age, I might have done better; however, since I wasn't, I compared myself to my classmates and concluded that I was "not smart."

This void has been the driving force of my entire adult life. To this day, my desire to "be smart" has led me to constantly read, write, learn, teach, and push myself to excel in any area that has to do with mental expansion. It is one of my strongest drives and it is responsible for what I have achieved in my business.

In addition, being so much younger than my peers, I was not accepted as part of any social group or clique. I was, without question, one of the most unpopular kids in my class and was always the last pick when we had to choose partners. I longed to be liked and to belong. Because of this, I place a high value on popularity and acceptance.

As you can see, my perceived voids clearly show my greatest values in life.

Can you see how the things you perceive as missing from your life are now a great value and a focus for you?

Abundance Thinking

Abundance thinking—that is, a just-in-time mindset—is much more balanced and congruent with the abundant universe we live in. With a just-in-time mindset, instead of thinking that everything good is in scarce supply so you'd better hoard it all now, you trust that everything good is readily available exactly when it is needed. A newer and more positive way to think can restore balance to your life. If you have been operating from a scarcity mindset, thinking in terms of abundance is a whole new way to look at things.

Even if you see yourself as having an abundance mindset, scarcity thinking can seep into your life and show up in forms you previously may have thought were unrelated. Look at your life right now: Do you have any undesirable excess in your life? If so, this might point to scarcity thinking in areas you have been unaware of. Clear up any scarcity thinking that may be unconsciously creating unwanted excess in your life. A mental shift is all that is needed to change your psychological settings.

Exercise: Creating a Mental Shift

Creating a mental shift is simple. The key point of the exercise is to see how you benefited from any lack you once perceived you had. This exercise gives you tangible evidence of the abundant universe we live in and shows you that there is never any lack.

Get out a paper and do this exercise:

1. When have you thought that you did not have enough of something? Write down at least ten memories. Next to each memory, identify how things worked out for you. Where did the abundance show up? Did it show up in the same form or a different form? In retrospect, how was abundance better? Write down the details.

    If what you felt you lacked was *time* to do a project, did the abundance show up in your creativity? Did someone step in to help you make up for lack of time? If you felt you lacked *money*, how did you make out, and where was the benefit? Did you make alternate plans, and did you get through it? Did someone step forth? Did you have a different experience than you expected and, if so, what did you learn from it?

2. Where in your life do you have abundance? List all the areas and all the things you feel you have more than enough of: things, friends, family, wisdom, and so forth. Answering this question will reaffirm that you do have abundance in your life. Write it down so you can recognize abundance in all the forms and in all the areas in which you have it.

    The most common complaint I hear is lack of money. Many people seem to recognize that they have a lot of everything except money. If you are one of them, I encourage you to view this in a different way. List everything you have that you consider valuable—material things, children, job, education, friends, health, etc. Next, put a dollar value next to each item so that you can see how much "money" you have in your life. If you want more money, you could just sell your things and convert them to money.

    Of course, you would never sell your children, but the point is to recognize that you actually do have abundance; it is just that not all of it is in the form of money. Viewing your situation in this light creates a new consciousness about money. Acceptance that stems from abundance, not from lack, creates balance and opens you up to creativity.

3. Keep a running list of all the synchronicities in your life, that is, all the things that showed up just when you needed them. For example, a friend called just when you needed to talk, a check arrived in the mail just in time to pay bills, the rain stopped and the sun came out just as you got out of the car. Note small things and big things.

Asking yourself a few questions about the areas in which you already *are* abundant and recognizing that things turned out okay even when you felt a scarcity helps the brain restructure. You can rewire your brain to expect more abundance.

Change your focus towards abundance and you will be amazed at how much abundance already surrounds you. Recognizing the truth about abundance will help you to release that old scarcity mindset you've been carrying around.

Struggle less, get more done, and experience the ease that accompanies just-in-time thinking!

Key Points

- A just-in-case mindset relates to scarcity thinking and limits us in many ways.
- A just-in-time mindset relates to abundance thinking and offers freedom.
- Scarcity thinking is caused by an unconscious belief that everything good is in scarce supply, which drives us to accumulate more and more.
- Scarcity thinking can be linked to excess weight, excess insecurity in relationships, and excess anxiety over money.
- Scarcity thinking is caused by fear of a void.
- Abundance thinking is the result of trusting that everything good is readily available exactly when it is needed.
- Voids drive us to value what we feel is missing and reveal our greatest values in life.
- Creating a mental shift from a scarcity mindset to an abundance mindset is simple and can be accomplished by focusing on the areas in which you feel you have enough.

FOUR

FOLLOW THE RULES OF THE ROAD

....

Align with universal laws for success and ultimate freedom.

....

Can you imagine the chaos you would see on the streets if no one followed the driving rules? What if no one paid attention to the speed limit signs or the traffic signs or other rules of the road? Imagine the chaos, as well as the wasted time and energy. If not for the rules of the road, we would be frustrated by the struggle to get anywhere safely and efficiently.

The Rules of the Road and the Rules of Life

Before you can drive a car and take off in the direction you want, in addition to learning how to drive, you must learn the laws of the road. The process is quite simple.

Getting to where you want to be in life, however, is not that simple. You may have a destination in mind, yet if you are unaware of the energetic laws governing life, the journey can be pretty challenging and confusing. Just as physical laws on Earth govern the physical and the tangible, universal laws govern the unseen world of energy.

Universal laws are spiritual extensions of physical laws, and they operate at all times. Universal laws govern all planes of existence and provide order to the universe in which we live. They are the basic, energetic building blocks of our world. If there were no universal laws, we would live in chaos. Universal laws exist whether or not we agree that they exist.

The Law of Gravity

You are already aware of some of the universal laws, such as the Law of Gravity. Gravity operates at all times. We know better than to fight with gravity, and we have learned to live with it because we recognize that it is part of our world. We know that if we jump from a window, we will not float to the ground, but rather land with a thud.

This most basic of universal laws provides you with a solid foundation for understanding how the universe works so that you can go with the flow of creation rather than struggle against it. This makes life more fulfilling, successful, and joyful.

Being unaware of any of the universal laws I will present here can be compared to going to a foreign country where you don't know the rules of the road. For example, if you have no idea that a specific sign is taking you in a direction opposite to the direction you want to go, you will never get there until you figure it out.

Seeing Is Believing Is an Outdated Adage

Many people still live according to the old saying, "Seeing is believing." It's natural for some to dismiss the unseen, claiming that things do not exist unless they can be experienced with the five senses.

Before the invention of the microscope, people would have thought you were crazy if you told them that creatures were crawling around on their skin. Today, we know that our skin is covered with 182 species of bacteria. Once science confirmed that bacteria on our skin could be seen, our frame of reference changed. We believe it because the microscope allowed us to see it.

We used to think the earth was flat until it was shown to be round. We thought the earth was the center of the universe until it was shown that the Sun is the center of our universe. At one time, we believed that the Milky Way was the only galaxy, but now scientists have proved that it is only one of *billions* of galaxies.

Now, no one questions the idea of using a small electronic gadget to talk to someone on the other side of the planet, let alone that this same gadget can hold thousands of songs, take pictures, and connect us to almost anyone or anything on something called the Internet. If you had predicted such a device even forty years ago, people would not have believed it. Our frame of knowledge at that time simply did not have the capacity to grasp it.

Our Frame of Knowledge Is Changing Rapidly

Our frame of knowledge is constantly changing as science unveils new truths. You have an advantage if you jump ahead of the times and affirm that something can be real even if it can't be verified with the five senses. So much is beyond the scope of our current awareness. For example, the universal laws are invisible, but if you live by them, you will see their positive effects in your life.

You may be wondering how many universal laws there are. Originally, according to Hermetic philosophy, there were seven. Subsequently, various numbers have been mentioned. Some say there are twelve universal laws and twenty-one subsidiary laws (*The Light Shall Set You Free*, 1998), and others say there are twenty (*Lighting the Light Within*, 1987). It seems no general agreement exists as to how many there are. What I will share here are those that I have found to be most helpful in understanding my own journey towards happiness.

The Law of Vibration

The Law of Vibration states that everything in the universe has an energetic vibration and its own vibrational frequency. Everything you see, feel, think, taste, and touch is vibrating and in motion—even if it appears solid. Science, through quantum physics, can now show us at the subatomic level that anything that looks solid is actually a sea of energy in motion.

You, as a human being, have a frequency that is different from everything and everyone around you. That is why you perceive that you are separate from what you see. At the deepest level, however, everything is connected in a unified field of energy. The unified field includes, but is not limited to, everything you see, everything you own, every relationship you have, every feeling you express, every thought you have, and everything you do. Every single thing in this universe has a distinct vibrational energy that defines it.

The Law of Vibration provides the foundation of the Law of Attraction, which you may already be familiar with. The Law of Attraction was the first universal law that became known to mainstream audiences through the book *The Secret* in 2006, which introduced the principle of "like attracts like."

How to make use of the Law of Vibration

Every person, situation, and decision in your life has an energetic vibration, and you are connected with it. Everything in your home has a vibration that appeals to you in some way. Everything you think, feel, and believe has a vibrational frequency, as well. The sum of everything you are, everything you do, and everything you have is what defines your vibrating point.

The effect of this law is most noticeable when you are going through a change. When you tire of a job, a relationship, or a piece of clothing and decide to do something about it, it is because your energetic vibration has changed and you no longer resonate with it. As you evolve and grow, you move your vibrating point to levels that attract different experiences into your life, experiences that match your new vibrations.

Understand that when you desire a new relationship or a new career, it is because a completion has occurred for you and your vibrating point has shifted. Perhaps you have learned a lesson or experienced healing or growth and are ready to graduate to a higher level of learning. If you feel you need to make a change, don't fight it and think you "should" stay where you are. Resisting the desire for change goes against your evolutionary nature.

Challenging situations

Let's say you are in a relationship and feel it is time for a shift, but you have children and fifteen years of history that is too painful to undo. Or, what if you are in a job that you know is not a match for you, but you have a mortgage to pay and no one to help you financially should you be unable to find another, more suitable job.

If you are still in that relationship or in that job, understand that you are exactly where you need to be. Yes, you may feel the need for a change, but you have not yet reached the threshold at which you know you *must* make a change. When you are ready, nothing will be able to keep you there. When it is "time," you literally will wake up one day and *know* that you cannot stay any longer. Until then, even if you want a change, trust that everything is exactly as it needs to be. Until your vibrating point shifts, you still have some things to complete in your current situation.

The energetic match with your environment

My feng shui work has shown me that homes have an energetic vibration. When someone is ready for a change, whether or not they are consciously aware of it, they nearly always feel the need to clear out a closet or clean up the house. They may not know why, but they just "feel like it." This indicates a vibrational shift to a higher level. In fact, they need the environment to better match their internal shift.

On a larger scale, every city, state, and country has a distinct energetic vibration. The people, culture, language, beliefs, politics, businesses, and so on, collectively create the vibrational feel of the place. That's why every place you go *feels* different. Sometimes, your energy may shift so dramatically that you no longer resonate with the city you live in and feel the need to move.

This happened to me while I was living in Japan after college. When I first arrived, I immediately fell in love with the culture, the people, and the language. I embraced everything Japanese and immersed myself in the experience of living there. I loved it so much that in my third year there, I declared to everyone I knew that I wanted to live in Japan forever. I resonated completely with everything Japanese and couldn't imagine that my feelings would change.

However, only six months after making that firm declaration, to my surprise, I began losing my connection to Japan. I felt as if I was "growing out" of living there. I still loved the people and the experiences, but for some reason I just *felt* it was time to move on.

I didn't know where I would go or what I would do, but a few days later, I saw a television show about Hawaii. It featured Konishiki, a famous sumo wrestler from Hawaii. I was mesmerized and felt the energy of Hawaii drawing me to visit. I had never been to Hawaii, so I immediately booked a vacation there. I didn't know what to expect.

When I stepped off the airplane, I *knew* I had to live there. Although I didn't know anything about the Law of Vibration at the time, I now can see that I felt an immediate vibrational match. That was in 1989. Within two months of visiting, I moved to Hawaii, and I have been in Hawaii for almost twenty-four years, now.

We are always exactly where we need to be no matter where we are in our lives, and whenever substantial inner work has occurred, we naturally feel compelled to find new circumstances to match our new state of being. Be open to recognizing your vibrational shifts as you lose resonance with the people and situations around you, and accept that you need to make a needed change.

Remember this law when you sense it is time in your life to make a big decision. Remind yourself that the answer will naturally come through a "knowing" as to when it is time. Otherwise you will spend a lot of time and unnecessary energy trying to know things that simply are not yet clear. Trust that when it is "time," you *will* be clear and will do what you have to do.

The Law of Abundance

Earlier, I talked about scarcity thinking versus abundance thinking and the importance of trusting in the abundance of the universe. If you did the exercise I suggested, you probably have seen how much abundance has always surrounded you. The Law of Abundance ties in with and supports the Law of Vibration.

The Law of Abundance states that prosperity is everywhere and that the abundance of the universe can be found in all forms of energy. The premise is that the universe provides unlimited options for anything and everything. Your energetic vibration determines what you attract, and what you attract comes to you in abundance. At its core, the Law of Abundance is the mindset of knowing that everything you need will be provided.

Look to nature, and you will see its abundance. In every natural element exists abundance, and nature effortlessly demonstrates the flow of abundance even during cycles of transition. When the seasons change, there is always enough to survive through the next harvest.

The Law of Abundance shows up as a range of extremes. What you believe about yourself determines where you are on that spectrum. Your self-worth determines your experience of abundance. The higher your self-worth, the more abundance you attract into your life. The lower your self-worth, the more lack of abundance you attract into your life.

How you can make use of the Law of Abundance

We need money to pay our bills, therefore many people mistakenly relate abundance only to money—and it's not all about money. Money is simply a form of energy that we use to balance the exchange of energy in the form of our talents, time, and gifts. If you do not value your time, talents, or gifts, you will not have abundance in the form of energy, and especially not in the form of money. Abundance is an energy that includes money, but is not limited to or determined by money.

Recognize your inherent value

Recognize that your time, energy, and talents have value. The more you value them, the more abundance in the form of money you can draw to you. For example, when I first started my astrological consultation business, I knew very little and had no experience. To reflect this, I charged thirty dollars per session.

Little by little over the years, as the value of what I had to offer increased, I naturally felt the need to raise my rates. The more time I spent learning about astrology and the more consultations I did, the more self-worth I felt when it came to my talent, knowledge, and skills. Now, ten years later, my fees are almost ten times my original fees. I have more abundance in the form of money because I recognized my value. This is an example of the Law of Abundance at play.

Are you worth it?

The key to abundance is to ask yourself if you are worthy of receiving it. See the abundance that you have so more can come to you. Use your expanding consciousness to see that an abundance of possibilities, options, and choices exist within all situations, relationships, and circumstances. Look at your challenges from a balanced and neutral place, and you will see unlimited ways in which a situation can change.

The Law of Cause and Effect

Every single action you take in your life has an effect, no matter how insignificant that effect may seem. As part of chaos theory, mathematician Edward Lorenz described something he calls the "butterfly effect," which says that when a butterfly flaps its wings in one part of the world, it can result later in a hurricane in another part of the world. In other words, a small change made now can cause a large-scale change in outcome over time.

The butterfly effect illustrates that everything we do has a profound effect on the world around us. In other words, one small movement has an effect on things we aren't even thinking about, and that is right in line with the Law of Cause and Effect.

This law states that every cause (action) has an effect, and every effect becomes the cause for something else. The universe is always in motion, progressing, and evolving from a chain of events, and for every action you initiate, there is an equal energetic effect.

This means that when you use your thoughts, actions, and feelings with high intentions, what you create not only goes out to others in the same manner, but also is returned to you. The same goes for when you use lower or more "negative" energies to create. The universe always returns what you have initiated. There are no coincidences, and everything you experience over time is in direct proportion to the causes you set into motion. This law is sometimes known as the Law of Karma.

When we were growing up, we all heard sayings like, "What you sow is what you reap" or, "The more you give, the more you receive." These sayings follow the order of cause (what we sow or give) and effect (what we reap or receive).

As an example, if your friend always dresses in overly revealing fashions yet complains that she only attracts men who are interested in sex and her body, she is blind to the cause. From an objective point of view, we can easily see that if she were to change how she dresses, she would create a different effect. She could simply ask herself what kind of effect she wants to create instead, and she would get an idea of how to change her cause (her style of clothing).

It is common to be blind to our own causes and operate in reverse by putting our focus on the effect instead of the cause. If you are challenged by a repeating pattern in your life, could it still be there because you have been focusing on the effects instead of the cause? Whenever you want changes in the results you receive (the effect) without considering the cause, you get nowhere, because operating in reverse goes against natural law.

How you can make use of the Law of Cause and Effect

Imagine that you are sitting in your own private movie theater and don't like the movie that is playing. Would you jump up and rip up the screen? Of course not. You would go to the projector and change the movie reel so you wouldn't have to watch that movie, anymore. Where in your everyday life are you ripping up the screen instead of altering your thinking or changing your actions? Where are you blind to the causes you are setting in motion?

Put your focus on the cause, not on the effect

About five years ago, Ophelia, a beautiful and successful woman in her late fifties, consulted with me about not having a partner in her life. She had been single for over ten years and said that although she had been looking, there was "no one" out there. She came to me to see what her astrology would say about the likelihood of love.

More important than any astrological concerns, I saw that she needed to shift her focus from the effect (no men) to the cause (what she was doing). I asked her what she was doing to meet appropriate men. She said that for many years, she had been an active member of several social and professional clubs. "There is just no one any good in any of them," she lamented. I told her to change where she hangs out (cause) so that she could meet a new set of people (effect).

I just found out last week that she immediately took my advice after that session. Lo and behold, she met someone within a month after joining a different social club. She has been living with him now for over four years. She changed her cause and, as a result, she changed the effect.

The Law of Cause and Effect for business enhancement

Let's look at using the Law of Cause and Effect to enhance business success. It goes without saying that most people go into business to make money and operate according to a "how-much-can-we-profit" mindset. Their theory is that, to be successful, you need to focus all thought, feeling, intent, and action on how to get more of a profit.

If you have a business and want to see increased profits, you can gain an additional advantage if you shift the focus of thought, feeling, intent, and action towards the *effect* you want people to feel as they experience what your business has to offer. In line with this law, when you focus on the *effect*, you will receive more profit-oriented ideas (causes) to help you to create that desired effect.

Concentrate on what you want to give or the effect you want to create. Put your energy into the effect, and you will find the answer to your cause. Remember the scarcity mindset I explained earlier? In accordance with the Law of Cause and Effect and the Law of Vibration, if scarcity dominates your thoughts, emotions, beliefs, and intent, you will attract limitation. By changing your cause and acting from an abundant mindset, you will see the effect of abundance.

Use the Law of Cause and Effect to discover life patterns that continually repeat themselves. Recognize the origin (cause), and you can choose a different action, trusting that a new effect will emerge.

Discipline is required

Discipline is part of using this law successfully. Notice your habits. What are their effects? Do you have habits you need to change? In what area of your life will greater discipline bring you more welcome effects? Action is not just a matter of taking physical action; it also refers to the actions inherent in your thoughts, emotions, beliefs, and intentions.

The Law of Compensation

The Law of Compensation, a corollary to the Law of Cause and Effect, states that each person is compensated in like manner for that which he or she has contributed. In other words, in the long run, you can never be compensated for more than you put in. Therefore, your effect will not be greater than whatever you put into your cause.

Receiving is as important as giving

The information about this law usually focuses on the giving aspect of the law: that is, give more to get more. However, many are very generous and give abundantly yet do not appear to be compensated in like manner. Why?

They have a hard time receiving because of low self-worth. Their low self-worth attracts experiences that reflect a "lower value," creating an imbalance. Unaware of this, they say to me, "I give so much to everyone—my time, my energy, my gifts and talents—why don't I have more in my life?"

The universe operates in perfect balance at all times. The two sides, in this case giving and receiving, must be in balance to create an equal and fair exchange of energy. One must not only give but also be able to receive. When you are able to receive (self-worth), you are better able to give (other-worth).

Self-worth equals self-wealth

Anytime you give something of yourself for nothing, you lower your self-worth. As Dr. John Demartini says, "It's your self-worth that determines your self-wealth, or what you'll allow yourself to be, do and have in life." Ask yourself how you can equalize and maximize your giving and receiving so that your self-worth and other-worth are equal and balanced?

How you can make use of the Law of Compensation

People say to me, "Alice, how can I charge for what I do? I love giving people advice and helping others." Maybe that is so, but are you tired at the end of the day? Do you complain about how everyone drains your energy? Do you feel unappreciated at times?

If so, perhaps you need to limit the time you spend offering advice to others. Maybe you need to accept help from others, as well, in order to balance the exchange? Re-examine how you are being compensated for your energy and ask yourself what is fair. If you give service that is valuable to others, are you receiving from those people service that is of equal value to you? Is it coming back to you in some form? Are you allowing yourself to "receive" it?

Anytime you give away something for nothing, you lower your self-worth.

You may be wondering about the Law of Cause and Effect and how it comes into play here. Wouldn't doing good "for nothing" come back to you in some form, even if not from the same person? Yes, it would, but ultimately, if you don't see yourself as worthy, you hold yourself back from what you could receive.

Raise your self-worth

When you offer a service to others, determine what would be fair compensation. If you provide a service to someone without predetermining a fair reward, you potentially lower your self-worth. That, in turn, not only lowers the value of the service you are providing, but it also creates an energy of uncertainty and obligation.

Payment does not have to be in the form of money, but there has to be some sort of exchange that is valuable to you. It could be appreciation, friendship, respect, or community status, but it is important to be conscious of what you are receiving for what you are giving.

Once you are clear about the value you offer and what you want in return, you free yourself from past or future obligations or complexities and you can be present in your life with no one owing anyone. By living this law, you inspire others to value themselves, as well.

Equal exchanges are balanced

Along the same lines, I have learned the value of never asking someone to provide something to me for "free," because it creates an imbalance in the relationship, as well as in your life. For a relationship to thrive and for you to be balanced in your giving and receiving, there always must be an even exchange of energy.

The Law of Relativity

The Law of Relativity gives us greater perspective on the journey of life, as well as on our path of growth and evolution. This law states that nothing is good, bad, big, or small until we relate it to something else. Everything in our lives just *is*—until we start comparing it. In other words, nothing in life has any meaning except for the meaning we give it.

You have your own unique journey and your own unique lessons. While the themes of our lessons may overlap, each of us moves through our lessons in our own way. You can't judge or compare who is better at learning their life lessons, because you live your life according to your own perceptions, experiences, and consciousness.

This universal law is about accepting yourself as an individual within the collective and recognizing that comparing yourself to others does not serve you because there is nothing to compare. The Law of Relativity is about accepting yourself as you are and accepting others as they are.

Many of us were conditioned in childhood to think that we should be the same as others; because of this, we compare and judge our beauty, success, happiness, finances, and love to what everyone else has. The purpose of life is to be ourselves, and yet we are taught to look to others to see how we measure up.

If you look back, you will see that you used all the knowledge and experience you had in every situation you encountered. Everything you did you did because of how you experienced the world *at that time.* You were simply being your best self, and then you learned to be more. Everything is relative to where you are at any given moment. Don't waste time or energy thinking that you should have done more or been more. Who says that where you are is not where you are supposed to be?

How you can make use of the Law of Relativity

Whenever you are feeling "less than," it is because you are comparing yourself to some person or some ideal. Whenever you are feeling "greater than," it is because you are comparing yourself to someone you are judging to be below you. Everything is relative.

You feel smart when you are talking to a "dummy," but you may feel like a "dummy" when talking to someone a lot smarter than you. You may think that making $50,000 a year is a pittance when you compare it to someone who makes over six figures, yet compare what you are making to the guy who is making $24,000, and you are making a killing. Appreciate where you are.

Use this law to help you accept yourself and others for who they are. Your free will determines where your energy goes, so honor yourself for the unique human being you are. There is nothing to compare and no need to evaluate your sameness. We all have our own paths according to the lessons we need to master. Accept *what is* as "perfection," and then use your power of choice to create the reality that you prefer.

The Law of Opposites

The Law of Opposites, also widely known as the Law of Polarity, states that everything has an opposite. We live in a universe of duality. Hot-cold, up-down, in-out, birth-death, happy-sad, mean-nice, etc., are examples of opposites we experience within ourselves, in our environment, and at every level of our lives. Opposites are necessary so that we can experience contrasts, and contrasts are how we grow.

Opposites are complementary aspects of the whole and exist at every level of our existence and being. Opposites exist in the form of feelings, characteristics, thoughts, beliefs, experiences, and more, and each cannot exist in balance without the other.

How you can make use of the Law of Opposites

Just as magnets have polarity—a north pole and a south pole—so also do we experience polarity in every part of our lives. We have successes *and* challenges, happiness *and* sadness, and good *and* bad in our lives. To expect that life will be otherwise is a setup for disappointment. This concept is the basis for finding the benefits of every challenge (Chapter One) and for understanding the importance of not judging events as either "good" or "bad" (Chapter Two).

In addition, look to the collective and you will see that balance is maintained at all times through opposites. For every viewpoint you have, someone somewhere has the opposite viewpoint. The Law of Opposites can be seen in full-blown action on the Internet—from beliefs about what is right and what is wrong to opinions about right or wrong actions. Remember, opposites exist to bring balance to the whole.

The Law of Seeds of the Opposite

This law is powerful when you can use it to view what you see as your successes and failures. In every failure, there is always the seed of success, and vice-versa. Thomas Edison literally failed a thousand times before creating the light bulb. When asked how he felt about failing so many times, he said that he didn't fail, but instead had learned 999 ways how not to make a light bulb. This way of thinking brought balance and enabled him to continue towards his success.

Walt Disney was fired by a newspaper editor because he lacked imagination, and he went bankrupt several times before he built Disneyland. Charles Shultz had every cartoon rejected by his high school yearbook staff, and Walt Disney wouldn't hire him. Michael Jordan was cut from his high school basketball team, and R.H. Macy failed seven times before Macy's department store caught on. All these people eventually succeeded as they recognized that the seed for success existed within their every failure.

How to make use of the Law of Seeds of the Opposite

Just as you can't have the crest of the wave without the bottom or the trough, you can't grow and expand without polarity. If your life is in a challenging place, look for where good exists and what you can learn from the challenges. While you are in the trough, you can organize, repair, reinvent, and prepare for the crest, because it will surely arrive.

If life seems to be going well, look for where you can do more and focus on that. By being aware of both sides of the polarities at the same time, you minimize oscillation and avoid the crashing waves of perceived failure. Goodness and success exist right alongside of difficulty and failure, and you grow by experiencing both.

As we were growing up, we were told what was good, bad, right, and wrong. Based on this, we judged our failures and successes using the same criteria. Decide for yourself what to focus on. Use this law to see that everything is possible. In every situation, always look for the seed of the opposite so that you can grow. The more you can be aware of the duality in your life, the happier your life will be.

The Law of Rhythm

The Law of Rhythm states that everything in the universe moves according to a pattern and has a natural cycle. Tides go in and out, night follows day, seasons change, and there is a new moon every twenty-nine days. This law reminds us that we will experience both good times and challenging times, and we will always have the opportunity to start fresh with a new cycle. Nothing happens randomly, and nothing stays the same forever. Change is constant. In every given moment, everything is either growing or dying.

Each of the four seasons builds on and supports the season before it. The rhythm of the seasons creates a cycle of growth and expansion that repeats itself every year. In the same way, every day, the sun rises in the east and sets in the west, and the moon appears each evening.

The Law of Rhythm provides a consistent circulation of energy to guide our lives. Since there is never a completion, the energy can move to higher and higher forms with each cycle. You can see this law in action in thousands of ways.

Astrological cycles

Planets move in defined cycles that can be tracked and directly correlated to world events as well as personal events, such as job changes, relationship shifts, health challenges, paradigm shifts, etc. Planetary movements track life cycles and give information about the timing of events that will unfold in our lives.

In my astrology practice, I have constantly seen this law in action. One year, transiting Saturn (planet of structure and responsibility) may hit a certain point in a natal astrological chart and prompt a promotion at work. The next year, the career move is old news. Instead, Uranus shows up (planet of surprises), and the client finds out that her husband suddenly wants a divorce. Her life is in a state of chaos as she does her best to navigate, wondering if she will ever find her center again. A few years later, Jupiter (planet of opportunities) and Venus (planet of love) cycle through her chart, and the client brings in her new fiancé and asks me when I can marry them.

Your life cycles

If you look back on your life, you will see repeating cycles. Saturn cycles show up every seven years, testing different areas of our lives and making us aware of where change is needed so that we can move to new levels. Through these cycles, we grow, heal, and reach new levels of power and awareness.

The Law of Rhythm confirms that our lives are not random and that nothing happens by chance. If you observe nature and the planetary cycles that are synchronous with your life, you will see that a divine order does exist, even in the seeming chaos and randomness we sometimes feel.

How you can make use of the Law of Rhythm

Use the Law of Rhythm to remind yourself that, no matter what, there is always another chance to learn a lesson, make changes in your life, or grow in new ways in order to become the best you that you can be. Everything moves according to its own rhythm and timeline, and you always have a chance to begin anew.

The Law of Transmutation

The Law of Transmutation is considered by many to be the first law of the universe, but I saved it for the end because it is especially good to remember during these crazy times we are living in. This law states that *change is all there is.* Change is energy's only attribute, and because of it, nothing is constant, even though sometimes we reminisce about the "good old days" and want life to stay the same.

How you can make use of the Law of Transmutation

When you experience change, know that it is normal. Change itself is normal. When you choose to make changes in your life, know also that this is normal. When you resist change, you resist growing, learning, and evolving. When you resist change, all you are doing is preparing yourself for something that no longer exists. In other words, since change is all there is, how you operated yesterday may not be the best way to operate today.

Accelerate forward

There is no such thing as going back, so accelerate forward by putting your focus on what you want to create in your life. The Law of Transmutation will always respond to your most dominant thought.

All Laws Work Together

All universal laws work together and build upon each other to create the components of your life. Let these laws be the foundation of your understanding. They will put you even more firmly in the driver's seat of your life. You are in control of shifting your life at any given moment, and everything you do makes a difference.

Key Points

- **The Law of Vibration**
    - Everything has an energetic vibration, even if it appears solid.
    - You perceive that you are separate from what you see because your frequency is different from everything around you, but at the deepest level, everything is connected.
    - The sum of everything you are defines your vibration point.
    - When your vibration point changes, you feel the need for external change.

- **The Law of Abundance**

  - Everything you need in life will be provided.
  - Your self-worth determines your experience of abundance. The higher your self-worth, the more abundant you feel.
  - Money is a form of energy that is used to balance the exchange of energy in the form of talent, time, and gifts.
  - To draw in more abundance, recognize that your time, energy, and talents are valuable.

- **The Law of Cause and Effect**

  - For every action you initiate, there is an equal and opposite effect, and that becomes the cause for something else.
  - If you don't like the effect, focus on the changing the cause.
  - If you want ideas for a new cause, clarify the effect you want.
  - Discipline is part of this law. Form new habits for success.

- **The Law of Compensation**

  - Every person is compensated in like manner for that which they have contributed.
  - When you give away something for nothing, you lower your self-worth.
  - Low self-worth holds you back from your ability to receive.
  - Determine fair compensation for everything you do in terms of money, friendship, appreciation, or respect.
  - To avoid feeling obligated, simplify your life, make sure there is an even exchange of energy in everything you do.

- **The Law of Relativity**

  - Nothing is good, bad, big, or small until you compare it to something else.
  - There is nothing to compare and no need to evaluate your sameness. We all have our own paths according to the lessons we need to master.
  - Accept yourself and others for who they are.

- **The Law of Opposites**

  - We live in a universe of duality, and the opposites are necessary for our growth.
  - The seed of success is in every failure, and vice-versa.
  - While you are in the trough of the wave, organize, repair, reinvent, and prepare for the crest.
  - When things are going well, look to see where you can do better to bring the balance.
  - Labeling something as good, bad, right, or wrong is a judgment. Decide for yourself what you want to focus on.

- **The Law of Rhythm**

  - Everything in the universe moves according to a pattern and has a natural cycle.
  - Nothing happens by chance, and nothing stays the same forever. Change is constant.
  - No matter what, there is always another chance to learn a lesson or make a change.

- **The Law of Transmutation**

  - Change is normal. Change is all there is.
  - Nothing is constant.
  - When you resist change, you resist growing, learning, and evolving.
  - There is no such thing as going back, so accelerate forward by putting your focus on what you want to create in your life.

- All universal laws work together and build upon each other.
- You are in control of shifting the direction of your life at any given moment.

FIVE

AVOID DISTRACTIONS

....

Don't let anything get in the way of your life.

....

"Keep your eyes on the road," is a vital rule to follow if you want to get to your destination safely or at all. Distractions abound, from other cars to backseat drivers to signs for coming attractions. In life, too, distractions abound, and distractions can keep you from living a life that you love.

If you love the life you are living and living the life that you love, distractions are not a big issue. No one gets distracted when they are doing something they really love to do. Have you ever seen a child who is playing video games get distracted? The only time distractions come into play is when you are uninspired by what you are doing or unclear about how you plan to get where you want to go.

A Modern Culture of Distraction

We live in a time like never before. Oceans of information are just a few keystrokes away and we are connected to each other through email, text messages, Internet articles, Facebook, RSS feeds, Twitter, and more. Everything competes to draw our focus away from any one thing. This is why it's more important than ever to get clear about what you want in life, adopt strategies and set boundaries. Distractions cease to exist once you define your focus.

Stop and think: you will be doing *something* until you die. Your waking hours will be filled with some type of activity or work, no matter where you spend your time, and this will continue in different forms through all the different stages of your growth and evolution. If you don't put some effort into finding out how you can live a life that inspires you, your whole life will end up being just one big distraction.

When you have a lot of *shoulds* going on in your life—"I should be doing this," "I should be doing that"—you are more prone to distraction. Why? Because no one is ever inspired by what they think they *should* do. Even if you think a *should* is high on your list of priorities, it really isn't, and that's why you get distracted from doing it. You only think it is a priority because you have talked yourself into it or been conditioned by others to think so.

There Is Only So Much Time

We have 365 days in a year, 24 hours in a day, and 60 minutes in an hour. There is only so much time to get things done. If your to-do list is filled with a lot of activity that does not inspire you, things you "gotta" do, and projects you have been procrastinating on, maybe it is time to relook at that list. How are you filling your time? Are there things you want to do but just can't get around to? Once you understand why you don't do those things and what you can do about it, you can focus on getting on with your life.

Wanda consulted me because she wanted to get her life organized. She had so much to do that it was weighing on her. When she did have time, she spaced out in front of the television or mindlessly surfed the Internet instead of using the time productively.

Wanda owned her own business, but she didn't need to be there every day because her husband took care of the daily operations. She had two teenagers and was in charge of running the household and attending to certain aspects of the business.

List All the To-Dos

To begin, I gave her two pieces of paper. On the first page, I asked her to write her actual to-dos and list all the things that she was responsible for over the course of a month. She listed things like cook meals, run the home, drive kids around, take care of the business, go to beauty appointments, exercise, and so on.

On the second piece of paper, I asked her to list all the things she wanted to do but was not doing. She listed 20-25 things: do a comparative business insurance analysis, scan and digitize all files, sell table and old furniture, clear out the closet, send product samples to distributors, set up a new computer, organize CDs, send out postcards to touch bases with old clients, and so on.

She wrote everything out, and we reviewed it. She was happy with the daily/weekly/monthly tasks she did, but she felt burdened by the projects and things to do she had listed on the second page. Some of those things had been on her list for literally two or three years.

Wanda's energy had been so tied up in the energetic heaviness of what she determined she had to do that she felt overwhelmed and used distractions as a "break." Even though she felt guilty, she just couldn't motivate herself to get going.

Delegate

Going through the items on the list one by one I asked her, "Can this be delegated, and to whom?" Her typical responses were that she didn't have anyone to delegate it to, only she could do it, or she didn't have the money to hire someone. I pointed out that her approach was not working and that sometimes it's wise to change up the strategy to get a different result. (Remember the Law of Cause and Effect?)

I suggested that she get an assistant she could pay hourly to assist her in doing the things she didn't want to do. Before she could protest about the financial limitations she had (which she was just about to do), I reminded her about the principle behind the Law of Abundance, that money is just a form of energy that can be used to exchange energy. I knew she would get reenergized and "get something back" if she did this.

Take action

The assistant she found helped her sell her table and furniture on Craigslist and send out "we miss you" postcards to old clients. Within a week, the mailings had reminded old clients to come back in and the assistant had sold most of the furniture, which gave Wanda extra funds. The assistant set up her computer, scanned the receipts, took her unwanted items to donation, and did all the other things Wanda did not feel inspired to do. Every day she felt better.

The items the assistant couldn't help her with were items that required specialized business expertise. Her original plan had been to figure out how to do these things herself to save money, however she had procrastinated for almost a year or two by then. She felt extremely guilty for being so lazy.

I suggested that she pay a business advisor to take care of the analysis so that she could lighten this burden that was getting heavier with each passing day. Within two weeks, she got the information she needed and made an insurance change that not only saved her money, but more important, lightened the energetic load she was carrying.

By delegating or hiring someone to do the low-priority things (things that weren't inspiring to her), she was able to focus on high-priority things in her life, such as creating a happier life for herself.

Your Turn

Take the time to do what I suggested for Wanda. List *everything* on two pages, with one page for actual to-dos and things you are responsible for over the course of a month and one page for all the things you want to do but are not doing. Breaking things down like this will give you objective clarity.

Ask yourself these three questions:

- Can I delegate any of this? If so, to whom?
- Do I need someone with specialized expertise to do this? If so, who?
- Do I need someone to hold me accountable? If so, who?

If you can't think of anyone that you know personally, use your networks! Post on Facebook or write to your email list that you are looking to hire some-one for a one-time project or possibly an ongoing project, what you can pay per hour, and ask whether they know anyone who would be interested. Mention that you are also looking for an accountability buddy (if you need one). You will be amazed at how much help there is if you reach out.

Put Everything in Your Schedule

If you don't schedule a task, it will not feel real to you. If you decide to wait until you "have some extra time," whatever you want to do will never get done. To make yourself accountable and prompt yourself to take action, you have to put it in your calendar. When it is in your calendar, if something else comes up, you will think twice before you change it. Remember this phrase: "If I don't schedule it, it's not real."

Create a Vision for the Future

One month later, Wanda came back for a follow-up session. This time, I gave her a sheet of paper titled, "What I Want My Life to Look Like in Two to Three Years."

I invited her to close her eyes, take a few deep breaths, and ask herself what she wanted. I asked her to see a vision she desired for her life. When she saw it, I asked her to write it down in detail. She listed all the major components of her vision. Beside each component, I asked her to write out three action steps she could do right away that would take her closer to what she wanted for herself.

Right Brain Plus Left Brain

When your right brain has generated an inspired vision or dreams for your life, you need a strategy for the left brain to follow. The left brain needs to understand how you will attain that vision. Without a left-brain strategy, it will take much longer for what you want to manifest, if it ever will. Long-term visions always need to be broken down into smaller action steps for the best success.

If you have the vision and the action steps, yet still can't seem to get going, it means that the *why* isn't big enough for you. In other words, you don't see why it is important enough to get you out of your comfort zone and into action. If this is the case, take 15-20 minutes to write down all the benefits you will receive by completing what you have been procrastinating on. When the *why* is big enough, you will have reason to get moving.

Tips, Tools, and Insights

Here are some tips, tools, and insights for getting more present with your life right away. Reframing and looking at things from a different perspective can bring new awareness.

- **Set yourself up right when you wake up.** The morning is an opportunity to plan. Either before getting out of bed or just before you turn on your computer, ask yourself: What is the one thing I can do today that will make my day highly successful? What is it that I can realistically accomplish that will further my focus and leave me feeling that I have been productive and successful at the end of the day?
- **Define your boundaries.** Now that we have smart phones, computers, and wireless Internet, our life lacks the natural boundaries of the old days, when home and work were geographically separate. We have unlimited options for working at home and communicating with others virtually anywhere, at any time. Although it may seem we spend more time working, we are far less productive than we think we are. Clearly, define when it is "work" time and when it is "play" time. This will keep you from getting distracted by play when you are working and vice-versa.
- **Set your intent.** Not having a plan for the day is like eating at an all-you-can-eat buffet without a plan. We tend to make poor food choices,

especially ones that are not the best for our long-term health goals. For example, unless we decide in advance that we will take only one trip to the dessert bar, it's likely that we will over indulge.

In the same way, throughout the day, we tend to get distracted by all the options around us. What do you care most about accomplishing today and in the near future? Set your intent and hold that boundary.

- **Stay connected with yourself throughout the day.** Set an alarm on your watch or phone to ring every hour or two. At the sound of the alarm, pause and ask yourself if you are doing what you need to be doing right now. You don't have to do this forever, but try it for a day or two. It will help you develop a habit of staying more in touch by "waking you up" every so often so you can check in.
- **Stand firm.** Only you know what you care most about accomplishing, so communicate this when others try to lure you off course. Say No politely but firmly (more on this in Chapter Ten). Instead of thinking, "Why not?" and saying Yes, think "Why?" and say No (graciously, of course). This simplifies your life and eliminates distractions.
- **Help yourself.** Our environment plays a big part in supporting our success, and often it dictates our actions. The people around you, the condition of your surroundings, as well as your mental and emotional space collectively make up your experience of your environment.

Make an effort to create an environment with as many components as possible that support your intent in life.

What Do You Really Want?

So far, I have introduced you to simple strategies that you can use to manage your life better in the short term. These will help you be more efficient in your day-to-day living.

In the long term, however, what's really important is having a deeper meaning to your life. If you don't define what you want in life and have a long-term vision, a purpose, or as Napoleon Hill called it, "a chief aim," each day will just blend into the next, and your life will roll into one, big, blurry, unmemorable distraction.

Everyone has dreams and desires, as well as a defined purpose for being here on earth. Over the course of our lives, we sometimes get sidetracked and fall away from who we are, and this makes us feel unhappy. If you are still searching for the bigger purpose of your life, I encourage you to make that one of your highest priorities.

I know that finding your purpose and what you want to do with your life can take a very long time. In fact, it is an ongoing project. It is something I work on every day. As I continue to grow and evolve, what inspires me changes. I have to continually ask myself what I want, otherwise I get caught up with things that are not really important to me.

Discover Your Purpose

It takes a lot of time, commitment, focus, and determination to discover your purpose, but the time to start is now. It is common not to know exactly what your purpose is. It is natural. Just allow yourself to experiment with different ideas and thoughts. Don't make the mistake of waiting until you are sure. Take risks, now. Explore different avenues of thought to see what can bring you closer to your powerful, inspired self.

Dr. Demartini suggests that you start by asking yourself three simple questions:

- What do I want to be?
- What do I want to do?
- What would I love to have?

Getting clear about why you are here opens up new avenues in your life. Answering these questions may seem tedious and your answers may seem shallow and pointless, however, the more you sit with yourself, the deeper within you will be able to go.

The more you can see your life and where it needs to be for you to feel happy and fulfilled, the more you will know what steps you need to take to get there. Deep inside yourself, you have the answers. Commit to yourself. Find out who you are, why you are here, and your life's purpose. There is no such thing as failure along the path of life. Whatever you do is simply an experience that informs you and leads you to the next step.

To be alert and live your life fully, you first need to be present with it—and you need to know why you are here. Where you find meaning, you will find inspiration. Your happiness depends on it!

Key Points

- Love your life and do what you love to do, and you won't get distracted.
- No one is ever inspired by things they think they *should* do.

- List all your to-dos on one sheet of paper and all the things you want to do but are not doing on another.
- Ask yourself what you can delegate, to whom, and whether you need someone to hold you accountable.
- Schedule things on your calendar to make them feel real and get them done.
- Combine vision (right brain) with strategy (left brain) for success.
- To get things done, your "why" has to be big enough. Write down all the advantages and benefits you will get if you do what you have been procrastinating on.
- Tips Tools and Insights to use right away:

  - When you wake up, ask yourself: What is the one thing I can do today that will make my day feel highly successful?
  - Clearly differentiate work time and play time and hold your boundaries.
  - Check in with yourself throughout the day.
  - Say No to whatever tries to lure you off course.
  - Help yourself by creating an environment that supports your intent in life.

- Getting clear about your life and your purpose opens up new avenues. Ask yourself these three questions suggested by Dr. Demartini:

  - What do I want to be?
  - What do I want to do?
  - What do I want to have?

SIX

REDUCE YOUR LOAD TO CONSERVE GAS

....

Regret and guilt are a waste of energy.

....

We have already talked about packing lightly relative to hoarding and scarcity thinking. To further conserve energy for your journey, let's see what else can be left behind.

Did you ever hear the story about the elderly monk who became the abbot of his monastery? After a lifetime of hand-copying many ancient texts, he realized that, for centuries, his order had been making copies of copies, so he decided to spend some time in the cellar examining some of the original documents.

Days later, the other monks became worried about his absence and went to look for him. They found him in the cellar weeping over a crumbling manuscript. He was moaning loudly. One of the monks asked him what was wrong, and he replied, "It says, "celebrate" not "celibate!"

Who hasn't looked back from time to time and wished that situations had been different or regretted making certain choices? We all have, and that's natural, but when we keep dragging the regret along and use it as an excuse for not enjoying the present, we lose out on living. If you don't unload regret, it weighs you down in the present and wastes the fuel you need for your journey towards happiness.

How to Let Go of Regret

You can't change the past, but you can change your story about the past. Examining your regrets from a different perspective provides opportunities to embrace new possibilities for expansion and growth. Clearing out regrets is like clearing out your closet. You look at the regret, decide you no longer want it to take up valuable space in your mind, and discard it.

Here is one method for letting go of regret:

Acknowledge the Regret

You can know you are using your regret about past events to stay stuck if you keep thinking, "I should have done it differently," or continually tell stories about how you would be skinnier, smarter, or have a better life if only you had done this or that. Acknowledge that, yes, although it's unfortunate that whatever it is happened, you are ready to move on.

Define the Type of Regret

There is "angry" regret and "sad" regret, and sometimes a mix of both. Clarify your regret. It is likely that both emotions are part of your regret to different degrees.

An example of a predominantly angry regret is, "I should never have trusted that lousy real estate agent and bought this house," or, "I lost half my retirement by following the advice of my financial adviser," or, "I regret the day I married her—she has caused me nothing but pain and suffering."

An example of a predominantly sad regret is, "My mother died before I could tell her I was sorry," or, "I wish I had worked less and spent more time with my children," or, "I regret not making the most of school when I had the opportunity."

Once you have defined the emotion as predominantly angry or sad, the next step is to list the reasons you are angry or sad about it.

Crystal's Regret

In Crystal's case, she had contracted the illness, ciguatera, at a Chinese restaurant over ten years before when she ate reef fish that she didn't know was contaminated with toxins. Immediately, her whole lifestyle had to revolve around having ciguatera. This disease affects the nervous and digestive system and doesn't go away, sometimes for dozens of years. It is painful at times, but mostly inconvenient. Ten years later it is still part of her story, especially when she has a breakout or an uncomfortable symptom.

She began by defining the regret as both angry and sad and wrote a list of how it is affecting her.

- I'm sad that I can't enjoy eating fish anymore without triggering a symptom.
- I'm sad that my skin breaks out in unpredictable rashes.
- I'm sad that I can't participate in the same activities as before.
- I'm sad that I can't indulge in alcohol like before without triggering discomfort.
- I'm sad there is no known treatment for ciguatera.
- I'm angry that the owners of the restaurant weren't more careful.
- I'm angry that my husband insisted we go there even though I didn't want to.
- I'm angry that I can't exercise as I did before.
- I'm angry that I have gained weight, because I look horrible.
- I'm angry that I have to limit myself in so many ways.

Listing the main emotional components of a regret, as Crystal did, makes it easier to move forward and let it go.

Grieve your sadness and acknowledge your anger.

Sadness is a natural reaction when you have lost something significant, such as a dream, an opportunity, a relationship, or a possession. Once you know exactly what you have lost, you can start healing.

Some regret is stubborn, however, and you have to consciously identify the sadness in order to grieve and heal. For the most part, Crystal had accepted her current lifestyle, however she still suffered from residual regret, and it was holding her back by keeping her stuck in the past.

Recognize what has been lost.

Nothing can change certain facts: she had gained weight, suffers from gastrointestinal discomfort, and has to be attentive to what triggers her symptoms. However, she can move towards acceptance by identifying what she feels she has lost.

Crystal realized that she most keenly felt the loss of two things: the freedom she once had to "do what she wanted, whenever she wanted" and her pre-ciguatera "shapely figure."

See what is lost in a new form.

When she looked for areas of her life in which she currently had freedom, she saw that she could now spend her time and money in ways she couldn't before because her husband's business had become financially successful. It is interesting that his financial success happened at about the time she contracted the disease. Looking at the situation afresh, she could see that she did have freedom, just in a different form.

She couldn't see ways in which she currently was beautiful, but she did realize that she was using the ciguatera as an excuse to be lazy. She saw that she could modify her diet if she wanted to. In this way, she took back responsibility instead of blaming the disease.

When analyzing your regrets, look for what you think you have lost and find where in your life you do have it. It may be hidden or in a different form.

Regret is a reminder, not a burden.

Don't let regret be a burden, but rather a reminder to grieve your losses, recognize there is no void, and move on. I hear people say that they regret certain choices they have made in life. They say that if they had taken a different path, they would be in a better place now. Whenever someone tells me they would have been better off had they married a different person, taken a different job, or not started their own business, I remind them about the experiences they have had because of the path they chose: the people they have met, the opportunities that came from knowing those people, and so forth.

You are in exactly the right place.

Remember, you are exactly where you need to be in your life right now. Everything that you did or didn't do has served a purpose. The alternate routes that play in your mind—what good are they? They do not result in you being where you are right now.

You are not further along, nor are you behind. You may think you are behind based on a judgment you have about your progress or unrealistic expectations you have for yourself, but the reality is, you are in the right place in your life.

The Paralyzing Emotion of Guilt

Are you holding on to guilt? When you are watching television, do you feel guilty that you are not folding the laundry? If you are folding the laundry, do you feel guilty for not taking the dogs out for a walk? If you are taking the dogs out for a walk, do you feel guilty that you are not returning all the emails that require a response? And if you suggest doing something that you want to do, do you feel guilty that you are not considering everyone else's opinions?

Guilt is like an inner watchdog that makes us feel bad if we don't do what we think we *should* do. In some cases, guilt is helpful; it can prompt us to rethink and realign our actions. However, most people I see make it excessively hard for themselves by holding onto a stubborn perspective that creates unnecessary guilt and stress.

What is Guilt?

Dr. John Demartini defines guilt as an emotion that arises when we unrealistically assume that we have caused ourselves, or others, more loss than gain, more drawback than benefit or more negative than positive. In other words, we have guilt because our perception of what we have done or not done is imbalanced. If we don't ever see the equilibrating gains, benefits, or positive aspects, of what we are judging to be wrong, we remain in a state of perpetual guilt.

One way to balance out your guilt is to stack up all the benefits of the actions you are taking (or not taking) that are making you feel guilty. This will change your perception. Using the earlier example, what are some benefits of watching television without folding the laundry, folding the laundry instead of walking the dogs, walking the dogs instead of answering the emails, or suggesting what you want to do instead of asking everyone else?

Seeing that every event or action has both a positive and a "negative" side brings in balance. If you don't make the effort to uncover a different aspect, you will continue to suffer.

Letting Go of Guilt

Many people have difficulty letting go of their day-to-day guilt, yet it can usually be neutralized by looking at it from a different perspective. Do you have any of the following types of guilt? Financial guilt, friend and family guilt, kid guilt, or "everything" guilt? How about green guilt, which is a modern-day guilt about not doing things that are healthy for your body or the planet.

If you are plagued by any of these guilts, here are some ways to shift your thinking about guilt:

Financial guilt

Do you feel guilty if you:

- Buy something frivolous for yourself?
- Get a beauty treatment that is not "necessary," such as a pedicure or facial?
- Pay more for something for convenience sake?
- "Waste money" by eating out all the time?

Remind yourself that money is a form of energy. Sometimes, we think of spending money as a "loss," failing to remember that the energy of the money is merely changing form. When you feel financial guilt coming on, ask yourself how the energy has changed form and in what way you have benefited. Do you feel better? If so, how did spending the money improve your mood? Boost your spirit? Save you energy?

Friend and family guilt

Do you feel guilty if you:

- Get invited to two events at the same time and have to turn one down?
- See someone you know but purposely avoid her?
- Get a birthday present from someone that you didn't give one to?
- Have a new, demanding job and miss momentous life celebrations?
- Secretly dislike certain members of your family?

Remind yourself that whatever you want, feel, or do is "okay." You experience guilt only when you judge what you are feeling as bad. There is nothing wrong with doing what works better for you or for valuing your time and energy enough that you avoid a potentially difficult situation. There are two sides to everything, and it is your responsibility to listen carefully to yourself and what you want without judgment. Ask yourself what you *want* to do instead of what you *should* do. There will be as many perspectives as there are people, when it comes to the right or wrong of what you are doing or not doing. You can't please everyone, and deep down, it never feels good when you betray yourself in order to please another.

As well, it is unrealistic to think that you will like everyone in this world, family or not, and will have the time or the energy to please everyone in your life. Choose to be self-centered, not in a snooty, it's-all-about-me way, but in a realistic way. Be authentic. You are who you are.

Guilt Trips Placed on Us by Others

I saw the following conversation in a comic strip:

A boy called his mother to see how she was doing. "Hi, Mom. How have you been?" he asked.

"Not good at all, son. I've been very weak," she said.

"Oh, no! What's wrong? Why have you been so weak?" the son asked.

"Because I haven't eaten for weeks," she replied.

"Oh, no, Mom! Are you sick? Why haven't you eaten?"

She replied, "Because I didn't want my mouth to be filled with food if you called."

Has someone ever said something that left you feeling guilty? It happens when we allow others to set the standard for what is "right." Then we feel bad for not following their agenda. The best way to handle this is to recognize that you can't please everyone, and everyone is responsible for herself. It is not your "job" to do what others want you to do, no matter who they are.

In the comic strip case, if calling once every two weeks works for him, then his mom eventually will have to take responsibility for herself and eat when she is hungry. Compromising and being creative in order to make it work for everyone is fine, but giving up "yourself" for another's agenda will eventually lead to resentment.

Kid guilt

Do you feel guilty if you:

- Take a yoga class instead of taking your child to a children's event?
- Buy fast food for the kids for dinner?
- Can't go to an important event for your child because you have to work?
- Let your child play video games so you can get some peace?

Know your priorities and remember that you are important, too. Sometimes, parents can get lost in thinking that being "good parents" means that they must sacrifice themselves, when, in fact, they just have to know their priorities. "June Cleaver" does not exist in real life. When you live by what you see as a priority, your children may not get what they want in the short term, but the bigger picture is that they are getting what you see as the overall best, whether that means you making more money, doing something that makes you happier and therefore makes you a happier parent, or doing something that saves time.

By showing your children that you respect yourself enough to stick to your priorities, you encourage them to set healthy boundaries for themselves as they go through life and become healthy adults. Any challenges they have because of your actions will further their maturity and growth and help them to see other perspectives. Don't allow your children to make you feel guilty. You are the authority and you are making choices that best serve your needs.

Free-floating guilt

Do you feel guilty if you:

- Mindlessly surf the Internet instead of doing something "important?"
- Eat a pint of ice cream before bed?
- Don't think you exercise as often as you *should?*
- Don't change the sheets every week?
- Fantasize about having a different life even though you love your family?

Be your own best supporter and limit your negative self-talk. What you do is what you do. What you did is what you did. Imagine that your friend told you the exact same thing about why she is feeling guilty. What would you say? You would likely talk her out of feeling guilty. We all tend to judge ourselves too strongly.

Next time you feel guilty about something, take yourself through these steps.

- Tell yourself what you would tell a friend.
- Find some benefits to balance out the drawbacks. What did you gain? More time? More energy? A mental break?
- Remind yourself that judging what you did is worse than what you did.
- Make new plans for tomorrow. Every moment is a fresh start. Take action to feel better. Schedule a workout, reaffirm what is important in your life, or apologize if you feel that you let someone down.

If you can't get through it on your own, call a trusted friend and talk about what you are feeling guilty for. Let them talk you out of it and give you advice. Everything is a choice. No one can make you feel guilty except yourself. You are the authority of your life, and only you can change your perspective on it.

Green Guilt

Do you feel guilty if you:

- Don't take action to recycle everything that is recyclable?
- Do less than you think you *should* to reduce your carbon footprint?
- Buy foods that are not organic or not local because they are cheaper?
- Love eating beef and pork?
- Drive a gas-guzzler that is bad for the environment?

Give yourself permission to get over it. Criticizing yourself for what you are not doing is not the way to get yourself to do it. In a perfectly balanced world, our actions would be ecologically loving and sound. However, you'll be happier if you realize that you can only keep up with what makes sense for you based on your priorities.

If you want to make living green a higher priority in your life, get some books and do some research on it. The more you understand what you can do and why, the more you will want to participate. "Guilting" yourself into doing it is not healthy, nor is it "green."

Instead of saying, "I should be doing X, Y, or Z to be more green," affirm that you will do it when you are inspired to do it, when it makes sense for you, and when it works for your life.

Move on from Regret and Guilt

With a little time, effort, and awareness, you can make a difference in the quality of your life by "simply" choosing to do so—without letting past actions in the form of regrets, or negative perceptions in the form of guilt, get in the way of your happiness.

Key Points

Regret

- You can't change the past but you can change the story you hold about the past.
- To let go of regret:

  - Acknowledge the regret.
  - Determine if it is an "angry" or "sad" regret.
  - Grieve your sadness.
  - Acknowledge your anger and look for the fear it is masking.
  - Recognize what has been lost and where you currently have it in your life, perhaps in a different form.
  - Let your regrets remind you to grieve your losses and move on.

- Remember you are exactly where you need to be in your life right now, and everything that has happened has served a purpose.

Guilt

- Guilt can be helpful when it prompts you to rethink and realign your actions.
- Don't make it hard on yourself by holding stubborn perspectives that create unnecessary guilt.

- Financial guilt can remind you that money is simply a form of energy. When you spend it, its energy comes back to you in different kinds of value.
- To alleviate friends and family guilt, remind yourself that whatever you want, feel, or do is "okay." You can't please everyone.
- To alleviate kid guilt, remember the bigger picture: your kids may not get everything they want in the short term, but overall they are getting the best that you can give.
- Whenever you start feeling guilty, limit your negative self-talk. What would you say to a friend?
- If you have green guilt, give yourself permission to get over it. You can only keep up with what makes sense for you. It is more important to maintain balance in your thinking and be your own authority.

SEVEN

DON'T DRIVE WHEN DROWSY

Take a break to realign, refresh, and reset.

When you have to drive tired, it is easy to slip into a life-endangering tug of war between your mind and your body. You know you need to stay awake, but your body just wants to sleep. If you nod off for a moment, your mind jumps in to wake you up. The best thing to do at this point, of course, is to pull over and take a break to refresh you.

On the journey through life, as well, it's important to take regular breaks from the stress of your physical, emotional, and mental worlds so that you can realign and refresh your connection with the spiritual. When you neglect to maintain your connection to the non-physical, you can get overwhelmed with life's challenges and forget that you have a bigger picture to consider.

Today's Increasing Demand for Spirituality

These days, more than ever, people are looking for a deeper connection to themselves and are more willing to embrace spiritual activities and pursue new avenues of self-discovery than in the past. Life is changing at a rapid pace, and anything that can help you get "in tune" is of high value.

Activities that once were considered "spiritual" practices that only a miniscule segment of the population (a.k.a. the "weirdos") participated in, have now become more common. Things like yoga, meditation, and gratitude journals are now acceptable to many as means of bringing increased levels of peace, harmony, and happiness into their lives.

Spirituality is a big topic these days. Google's keyword tool shows that that 2.8 million people per month search Google for answers on "how to be spiritual," demonstrating that curiosity about universal spiritual practices is a rising trend. Just three years ago, that number was only 1.9 million.

Even some workplaces have embraced the trend. Google teaches yoga and meditation techniques to their 30,000 plus employees on an optional basis. They also provide space where employees can meditate. Zappos brings in inspirational speakers and teachers of spiritual practices to help interested employees engage in spirituality.

Connecting to Spirituality

We human beings have four bodies. We have a physical body that we use as a vehicle to move through life. We have an emotional body that we use to "feel" with. We have a mental body to think and reason with. We have a spiritual body to connect us to our essence, to our inspiration, to our purpose here on earth. The spiritual body is also referred to as our soul, our intuition, our greater consciousness, our higher self, and our inner voice.

So, as four-bodied beings, when we get too caught up in the physical, emotional, and mental bodies, we can feel like a hamster on a wheel, constantly moving but going nowhere. By embracing the spiritual part of us, we not only expand and grow, but we bring more balance and a new perspective to our existence. Engaging our spiritual body can help us to live with a greater sense of awareness, and as a result, to operate at our fullest potential.

What It Means to be Spiritually Connected

Each of us has a spirit, an essence that is uniquely ours. Being spiritually connected means, literally, being in touch with your spiritual self, which will increase your understanding of your life journey, which is as unique as you are. When you stay connected to this part of yourself, you trust life more and are less afraid of the unknowns. Through this connection, you will naturally gain a sense of knowing that you are part of an incredible network of synchronicities, meaning, and purpose.

The Benefits of Connecting to Your Spiritual Self

Nowadays, our daily lives can get quite hectic. The more we have on our to-do lists, the easier it is to focus on the external world, where we get caught up in working harder and harder to make things happen.

If you establish a spiritual practice that turns your focus inward, you create a means by which you can build a better connection to your spiritual self. As a result, over time, you will gain peace, clarity, relief from stress, and a greater sense of ease in your everyday life. As well, you will increase your ability to hear the guidance of your inner voice, the voice of your heart.

What a Regular Spiritual Practice Is

A regular, preferably daily, spiritual practice is a habit you choose to form by creating a sacred space and a defined time to incorporate activities and tools that make it easier to connect to the spiritual. A regular spiritual practice gives your mind, body, and emotions a rest. It is a time you set aside to *be* rather than *do*.

A spiritual practice is a way to explore and experience the depths of your spiritual self. It is a highly personal pursuit and a life-long process. Do what works best for you based on your lifestyle, work habits, family situation, and available time.

Create a Practice

Consider the following:

When? You can do a practice as little or as often as you want, however, make it a regular recurring appointment that you schedule, just as you would schedule an exercise session with a trainer. Decide on the time of day. Will it be morning, during the day sometime, or during the evening? Put it in your calendar, and I mean that literally.

Where? Choose a place based on where you will be at the time you have decided, a place in which you will have the least possibility of distractions, interruptions, and noise. If possible, clear out all clutter and unnecessary items and display items that are beautiful and inspiring.

How long? The length of time does not matter as much as your intention and follow-through. You can start with ten or fifteen minutes and increase it as you experience the benefits.

What? You can choose to listen to music, read an inspirational book, journal, write letters of gratitude to people you appreciate, light candles, meditate, read or write affirmations, write down your worries, pray, contemplate nature, visualize a goal or an outcome, talk to your guides, unplug from stress, write down what inspires you, develop a purpose statement, breathe, stretch, etc.

Why? To be consistent with your practice, you need to know why you are doing it. What do you want to get out of maintaining a practice? How will you benefit? What will these benefits lead to? If your *why* isn't big enough, you won't continue the practice. Know why you are doing it. Write down twenty to thirty benefits of doing a spiritual practice. This will inspire you to begin.

Basics When Doing Your Practice

As you begin your practice each time, here are a few things that will be helpful to keep in mind:

Set your intent. When you sit down, have an intention in mind for what you want to accomplish during the session. For example, it could be to de-stress, to receive insight on a problem, to hold a friend or family member who is challenged in a positive light, to learn something new, or to get inspired by something. Whatever it is, when you sit down, be sure to set your intent.

Get connected. Take a deep breath and focus your attention inwards. Consciously choose to be receptive. Most likely, your energies are focused outward for most of the day, so this will be a great break and vital to bringing balance to your life.

Let go. Once you have set your intent for the session, let go of expectations. Commend yourself for setting aside the time, removing yourself from external distractions, and keeping your commitment. After that, just let go.

Other Ways to Connect to Your Spirituality

People have asked me whether they "have to" establish a practice in order to get spiritually connected. Fortunately, there are countless ways to connect to your spirituality without having to make a regular practice. Here are my favorite ways to invite spirituality into my life. You can do them any day, any time.

Get quiet and breathe. Turn off phones, computers, and televisions and sit quietly outdoors or indoors. Close your eyes and breathe in and out slowly. You can do this for five minutes or fifty. Connect to the life force that keeps your heart beating and allow it to bring you to a humbled and more relaxed state. You can call it meditation or you can call it "getting away." Either way, it will refresh you and get you ready to get back into your life.

Count your blessings. This is simple, but effective. Being thankful and appreciative not only gives you a greater sense of well-being, it also opens you up to growth and expansion. Focusing on what you appreciate can help you feel more spiritually connected. Close your eyes and say thank you for your joys and your challenges. Make a list. Seeing the things you are grateful for on paper makes this exercise even more powerful. Make a list that accumulates in your journal.

Choose to make an attitude shift. Life is not always easy, but your attitude about it makes a big difference. Take a moment to think of a challenging person or situation and make the choice to see the person or situation differently and respond differently. When you commit to seeing a different perspective, you will feel spiritually expanded even if you can't change the outcome.

Find out what inspires you. When we are inspired, we feel uplifted and renewed. If you haven't done something inspiring lately, find something you love to do. If you don't know what that might be, commit to exploring. Don't wait. If you wait until you have more time or your problems go away, it will never happen. People who are inspired by life are experiencing the essence of spirituality.

Surround yourself with inspiring people. If the people you hang around with bring you down, actively search for new people to surround yourself with. Join a class or a group. Search for communities of like-minded people. Find people who match who you are now, not the person you were in the past.

Open yourself up to experimentation. If your method of seeking spirituality is falling flat, try something different. Go to a Buddhist dharma talk, a Unity Church meeting, a synagogue, an evening of fire dancing, or a full-moon drumming night. Try out things you may never have thought to try and see what helps you feel connected to your spirit. You may meet some very interesting people, as well.

Spend time in nature. Surround yourself with the beauty of nature. Feel the presence of divine consciousness as you gaze at the mountains, ocean, desert, lake, trees, flowers—or whatever of the natural world surrounds you. Contemplate how incredible it is that we live in such a beautiful world. See the peace and strength in nature and allow it to inspire you.

Say a silent prayer. Prayers are not only for when things are going badly; they are also excellent for times when your life is going well. Pray to your higher self, your spirit guides, your angels, the Creator, the Universe—anyone or anything you want. Pray for yourself, your family, and loved ones. Speak words of thanks aloud or just think the words in your head. It is extremely powerful to say a blessing for anything, anyone, or any situation.

Read spiritual, inspirational, and enlightening books. Keep spiritual books around the house and at work, and keep one in your briefcase or handbag. When you feel like it, take a few moments to read and reflect. Reading inspired words can be very uplifting, especially during times of high stress. Create the opportunity, and the right words—just what you need to hear—will come forth exactly when you need them.

Keep a journal. Buy a nice notebook, one chosen especially for your notes of appreciation and your commitments to yourself, and write anything and everything in it. Journaling is a great outlet for focusing on the positive aspects of your life and steering yourself away from downward-spiraling thoughts.

Find What Works for You

We human beings are here on earth to grow and evolve and, in the process, find love and joy. All of our experiences, both the positive ones and the negative ones, help us to keep reaching new levels in our lives. Life is especially difficult, though, if we feel that we experience more negatives than positives.

This is when doing something "spiritual" or developing a spiritual practice can help. Try out the things I have mentioned. When you find something that resonates with you, you reboot and set an intention to connect with a new perspective or with something that is "positive" in the greater picture of your life.

Key Points

- Take regular breaks from the stresses in life and refresh your connection with the spiritual so you don't get overwhelmed with life's challenges.
- Human beings have four bodies: physical, emotional, mental, and spiritual.
- When we are connected to the spiritual aspect of ourselves, we trust life more and are less afraid of the unknowns.
- Establishing a spiritual practice will, over time, give you peace, clarity, relief from stress, and a general sense of greater ease.
- A spiritual practice is a habit formed when you create a space and dedicate time to *being* instead of *doing*.
- To create a practice, decide when, where, how long, what, and why you want to do it. If your *why* isn't big enough, you won't continue your practice. Inspire yourself to begin by writing down twenty to thirty benefits of doing a spiritual practice.
- When doing your practice, set your intention, get connected by focusing inward, and let go of expectations.
- You can also connect to your spirituality without making it a regular practice by doing any of the following:

- Get quiet and breathe.
- Count your blessings.
- Choose to make an attitude shift.
- Find out what inspires you.
- Surround yourself with inspiring people.
- Open yourself up to experimentation.
- Spend time in nature.
- Say a silent prayer.
- Read spiritual, inspirational, enlightening books.
- Keep a journal.

- When you find a practice or activity that resonates with you, you reboot and set an intention to connect with a new perspective or with something that is "positive" in the greater picture of your life.

EIGHT

WATCH OUT FOR YOUR BLIND SPOTS

....

Unlearn past lessons that keep you from moving
forward with clarity.

....

Virtually all vehicles have blind spots, and being unaware of them definitely increases our chances of having an accident. Blind spots on the journey to happiness similarly increase the likelihood that we will have life accidents and other difficulties that we might have been able to avoid. These blind spots arise out of some of the lessons we learned while growing up that hinder us as adults.

Lessons Learned Blindly

When I was a child, the adults in my life often repeated this advice in some form: "Learn your lessons now while you're young, and you will be successful." When they were upset, they would change it to: "You'd better learn your lesson from this!" said while shaking a finger in my face. They all were intent on teaching me the "lessons" of life—and they did their job well, because some of those lessons definitely helped me.

Our life lessons took us a long time to learn—decades, in fact! During this time, we learned from the adults around us how to act and how to think and move through life in order to be successful. These lessons were cemented through repetition and sometimes punishment; as a result, they were ingrained in our psyches. While some of the lessons were helpful, many hindered me until I was able to recognize the value of "unlearning" them.

I call the lessons that hindered me "blind" lessons because I learned them and followed them blindly until I realized that I could "unlearn" them.

Blind Lesson: What People Think About You Is Important.

When I was ten, I had a friend named Jill. She was my best friend, and I wanted to hold hands when we were at recess for no other reason than I liked her. One day, she said, "We have to stop holding hands." When I asked her why, she said, "My mother said that people are going to think we are gay." I didn't understand what that meant or why it even mattered what people thought, but it mattered a great deal to Jill's mom, so we stopped. I missed holding Jill's hand.

When I was twelve, I had a shirt with a big, red, hairy-looking heart design in the middle of it, and for some strange reason, I fell in love with how it looked on me. I insisted on wearing that shirt at every opportunity for months until it fell apart. Whenever my mom caught me wearing the shirt for too many days in a row, she scolded me with some variation of, "Change your shirt! People are going to think that we have no money to buy you clothes," or, "People are going to think that I never wash your clothes," or, "People are going to think we don't take good care of you."

Eventually, I was forbidden to wear the shirt more than once a week because of "what people would think." I still found a way to wear it every day. Either I hid it under a zipped-up jacket, took it from the laundry hamper (yes, and wore it dirty), or sneaked it into my backpack to change into when I got to school. The only thing that mattered to me was the fact that I liked the shirt, and I didn't understand my mom's reasoning. Obviously, I was unaware of the importance of "what others thought."

Well, the shirt fell apart, but all too soon, I too began to believe that what other people thought was important. I learned to tailor what I said and did so I would be "accepted" by society and "others," especially those I wanted approval from. The result of this blind lesson I learned so well was that, for most of my adult life, I cared too much about what others thought.

New Lesson: Who Cares What People Think!

If you find yourself saying, "I don't want people to think I'm…" you've got a blind spot. Now, why should you disregard what others think? Because, no matter what you do or don't do, people will have opinions about your actions, and those opinions quite naturally will be based on *their* perspective, not yours, regardless of whether they can see your point of view.

I learned this lesson partly through the Internet. From time to time, I Google my name to see what is being said about me in regards to my business and the services I offer. Usually, it's nothing unexpected or out of the ordinary, however in one particularly memorable case, I read a post where someone wrote a detailed account about how cold, unfriendly, and arrogant I was—and below that, others posted their agreement!

This was a wake-up call. Now, whereas I'm sure I can occasionally be cold, unfriendly, and arrogant, the truth is that I make a conscious effort to be warm, friendly, and amicable at all times, and especially in public. After all, I don't want people to think I am cold, unfriendly, and arrogant! With a sigh, I realized that others will think what they want to think and see what they want to see, no matter what I do or don't do.

This leads to a question you can ask yourself: Does it *really* matter what others think? Imagine what you would do if what others thought didn't matter to you in the slightest. Act on it soon, because in the long and short of it, you are the only one that matters.

Blind Lesson: Loss Is a Bad Thing

Last night at dinner, I had an interesting conversation with Mike Irish, a gentleman in his fifties who has been in one of my social circles for over ten years. I didn't know his background, only that currently he is an established businessman here in Honolulu with a favorable reputation. On the few occasions that we talked in depth, I had noticed his appreciation for his life, his family, his employees, and the community. His outlook always seemed positive, no matter what "stresses" were going on, and I loved that about him.

In a group conversation, the topic of appreciation came up. Mike mentioned that he is thankful for the losses he has experienced because they are what give him profound appreciation for what his life has to offer today. I asked about those losses, assuming they were business related, and he told me his story.

In 1971, he was eighteen years old and playing football for the University of Hawaii. An injury during a scrimmage left him flat on his back, unable to feel or move his arms or legs. He wasn't worried; he thought it was just a "stinger" (a term he and his teammates used when sudden physical impact led to temporary numbness). He was sure that eventually he would regain feeling and movement. At the hospital, however, tests showed that he had broken his neck and severed his spinal cord. He was told he would be a quadriplegic and never walk again.

The doctors told him that he was lucky just to be alive. Immediately, he lapsed into a self-induced coma.

When he woke up and realized that he was, as he put it, "nothing but a head," he went through various degrees of sadness, anger, and depression. No matter what anyone said, all he wanted was to die. He even tried unsuccessfully to end his life by holding his breath until he passed out only to wake up again to his depressing reality.

A miraculous recovery

One day, six months later, he felt some "weird sensations," and doctors soon discovered that his spinal cord wasn't completely severed as they had thought. Some of his nerves started firing again, and he entered a rehab program to work towards recovery. Within two years after the accident, he had learned how to walk, run, move, and function again. Doctors said his case was "one in a million."

The moral of the story

In Chapter Four, I talked about the Law of Relativity: Nothing is good, bad, big, or small until you relate it to something else. We can see this law at work in Mike's situation: to the degree that life was limiting for him while he was "just a head" is the degree to which he now experiences and appreciates the freedom that life offers. This explains why his view and appreciation for life are so different from those of the average person who has not experienced Mike's magnitude of loss.

While losses can, in retrospect, cause us to appreciate what we have in the present, as in Mike's case, losses also open the path to more in our lives, not less, as we have been taught. Many of us fear loss because, at some level, we believe that losing something brings a negative outcome.

New Lesson: Losses Lead to Gains.

Adopt this lesson if you are resisting the loss of something in your life—a good situation, a relationship, finances, your health, your status—or if you find that you are taking action just to avoid loss. Loss is only a "bad" thing to the degree that we fear or avoid it.

Losses are part of the natural cycle of life, and when you can see them relative to the bigger picture of your life, they are not as devastating as you may think. Losses are part of the natural cycle. Trees lose their leaves so they can bring forth new leaves and bear new fruit. Situations and people and things pass out of our lives so that we can grow and produce even more for ourselves. See The Law of Rhythm in Chapter Four for more on this theme.

Take a moment to look back on a loss you experienced and see if you can connect it to a direct gain that came out of that loss. It may be in a different form and hard to recognize, but the gain is always there. You may have lost a job or a friend only to find a different job or new friends. You may have lost your mate and gained the support of more friends and eventually a new partner; on the other hand, you may have gained the gift of time to focus on yourself. You may have lost money in a bad investment but gained a different outlook, new strategies, and a fresh focus.

We all experience losses, and we all continue to expand and grow throughout life. Adopting the outlook that "losses lead to gains," puts you in control; you can relax, knowing that you can never, ever lose in life. There is a gain for every loss.

Blind Lesson: Failure Is a Bad Thing.

The most frequently asked questions I get from new clients who come in for an astrological consultation concern success: "Can you tell whether my career change will be successful?" or, "Will this new relationship work out?" Without even looking at the chart, my answer is always, "Of course!" Why? Because I know that no matter what they may perceive as a possible failure (financial loss, co-worker challenges, eventual relationship loss, or giving up good career benefits to take a chance), ultimately their success will be built on it.

Failure or success?

Hawaiian Regional Cuisine Master Chef Alan Wong, whose Honolulu restaurant is consistently ranked in the top ten nationally by magazines and food critics worldwide, opened up a new concept market in 1999 and named it the Hawaii Regional Cuisine Marketplace. Although a lot of creativity, time, money, and energy went into this venture, it closed less than two years after its doors opened due to a lack of customers to keep it in business.

At the time, Wong's company took a great financial hit and the venture was seen as a business failure. Yet, today, he says it was a key component on which his current success is built.

The financial investment he made in the marketplace tied him up for years and prevented him from expanding. This, however, gave him the opportunity to work on his company culture and concepts, establish his standards, and perfect his cuisine, management, and business skills. He put his focus on building his brand, and where others were expanding and diluting their businesses, he was distilling his. It forced him to limit himself in many ways that prepared him for expansion in later years. The advice he gives his management team is, "Failures are key ingredients in the recipe of success."

Not trying at all is failure.

Chef Wong also says, "Our successes are built on our failures, and the biggest failure is not trying at all." He explains that life has a funny habit of knocking you down, but when you are down, you have a choice; you can do one of three things:

- You can give up.
- You can get up and do the same thing (which will give you the same result).
- You can get up and make a change.

Over time, the changes you make contribute to your growth, success, and who you are today. Not only do you become a better person, but you also become better at handling life when you "expect" that it will knock you down and anticipate that you will get up and keep adjusting. According to Chef Wong, there is no such thing as failure, and it doesn't matter what happened, who did what to you, where it happened, or how they did it. Your success is determined solely by what you do after the thing has happened.

Why we fear failure

We fear failure not only because we have been conditioned to think that we must avoid it, but also because we think that failure makes us look bad: "What will others think?" When we fail, we feel we have done something "wrong." We think that failures confirm to the world that we are unsuccessful, and so we avoid them at all costs, not recognizing that failures are jewels in disguise. See the Law of Opposites in Chapter Four for more on this theme.

New Lesson: Successes Are Built upon Failures.

Success is not the opposite of failure as most people think. From losing weight to learning how to ride a bike, we succeed to the degree that we try, fail, and learn. Think about it. Everything you have improved upon in your life has likely come from a "failure," large or small. Your successes are built upon your failures. We learn from our failures. Failures are the stepping-stones leading to expansion and growth.

Studies have shown that the more relaxed people are about the possibility of doing poorly at something, the easier it is for them to do well. Alternatively, people who worry about "not getting it right" literally shut down their ability to "get it." So, from now on, affirm that failure is a key component in your success and you can't go wrong.

Unlearning Lessons Learned Blindly

When you are considering whether you may need to unlearn a particular lesson, take a moment to think about why that lesson in its current form may be holding you back. As you begin to question a lesson learned blindly, your brain will begin to release its hold on it.

For example, let's consider "What will people think?" Why don't you want to make decisions for yourself based on what other people think?

Could it be because it suppresses your authentic expression? Does it give others power over you and snuff out your originality? Does it lead to resenting yourself and others? Does it negatively reinforce your low self-esteem? For every lesson that you want to unlearn, think of a few reasons why it would be better to unlearn it.

Small Changes Lead to "Unlearning"

As they say, every journey starts with a first step. If "unlearning" resonates with you, start implementing change every morning with some simple actions that can get you on the path to breaking patterns even before you get to work. Initiating small changes in your physical world prepares you for the emotional and mental changes needed to unlearn some outdated lessons.

Here are ten simple ways to start:

Go to sleep earlier so you have at least fifteen more minutes of sleep than usual.

- Use a different alarm clock or a different alarm sound to wake you up.
- Close your eyes when you shower and feel your senses come to life.
- Brush your teeth with a different brand of toothpaste and with your opposite hand.
- Part your hair in a different place, or wear it in a different style.
- Wear items of clothing you rarely wear instead of the ones you always reach for.
- Watch a different news channel than usual or read the paper from back to front.
- Drink tea instead of coffee or vice-versa.
- Have a completely different type of breakfast (preferably healthy).
- Drive a different route to work.

Unlearning Is a Way to Experience More

It has become increasingly apparent to me that our ability to find joy doesn't depend on how well we learned our lessons in the past, but on how well we are able to unlearn them as we move into the future. Today, with information coming at us from all directions, we can get caught up in thinking that the only way to grow is to keep assimilating new knowledge.

Not so! *Unlearning* is also a great way to experience "more" in your life. What are some lessons you have learned that you would gain something from unlearning? Remember, no matter where you are in life, as long as you are learning, it is never too late to unlearn!

Key Points

- Some lessons we learned blindly as children hinder our happiness until we "unlearn" them.
- Unlearn "What people think is important." Replace with "Who cares what people think!" No matter what you do or don't do, people will have opinions about your actions based on their own perspectives.
- Unlearn "Loss is a bad thing." Replace with "Losses lead to gains." Many of us fear loss, but in the bigger picture, losses open our lives to more, not less.
- Unlearn "I don't want to fail." Replace with "My successes are built on my failures." Success is not the opposite of failure; we succeed to the degree that we try, fail, and learn. Studies have shown that the more people worry about "not getting it right," the more they shut down their ability to "get it."
- When you question a lesson that is not serving you, your brain will begin to release its hold on that belief.
- You can prepare for the emotional and mental shifts needed to unlearn outdated lessons by initiating small changes in your daily life, such as changing the sound of your alarm, taking a different route to work, or watching a different news channel.
- Our ability to find joy doesn't depend on how well we learned our lessons in the past, but on how well we are able to unlearn them as we move into the future.

NINE

DON'T FOLLOW THE DRIVER
AHEAD TOO CLOSELY

....

Be your authentic self—and no one else.

....

'm sure you know the hazards of following another driver too closely: the car you are following could turn into a brick wall in an instant. You may not realize it, but you are putting your life into another driver's hands, and you may not like the outcome. It is not so very different from trying to be what others expect you to be in order to feel accepted. How can you be happy if you are giving your life away to fulfill others' expectations? How can you be happy if you are not your authentic self?

Losing My Identity in Others

When I attended high school in Taiwan, there was a boy in my ninth-grade class named Jeff. He was funny, charismatic, popular, engaging, and he could tell wonderful stories. Over the years, he grew to be loved by everyone, students and teachers alike. He was fun to be around because he was inspired by so many things and he talked about them incessantly. He loved the movie *Star Wars*, sports cars, designer labels, the latest gadgets, soap operas, and music. Anything he thought was "cool" became the "in" thing, and everyone who wanted to be cool wanted it.

Back then, words like *authenticity* and *inspiration* were not part of my vocabulary. In hindsight, though, I realize that people were drawn to Jeff because he was authentic and inspired. We all want to be inspired by something, and it was easy to get caught up in the wave of his joyful outlook.

By my senior year, Jeff was my best friend. We both left our families in Taiwan to attend the same university in California. We knew no one at the new school we went to, so Jeff became like family. He was like a brother I looked up to, and I happily followed him around.

So that we could still hang out together, his hobbies became my hobbies, his interests became my interests, and the friends he made became my friends. I felt secure when I did the things Jeff liked, wore clothes he thought were cool, and bought the things he thought were cool. I didn't really know what I wanted, anyway, so it was easy just to follow along.

I took windsurfing and surfing classes even though I didn't like being in the water; I subscribed to *Car and Driver* magazine even though I didn't know how to drive at the time; I put up car posters all over my dorm room, bought the latest gadgets, got good at playing video games like *Pac-Man* and *Centipede,* and watched soap operas daily, and all because Jeff did. I was trying to assure that he and others would accept me.

Jeff was not the only person I followed too closely behind. My dad had wanted me to be a doctor for as long as I could remember, so I took the pre-med route in school. He also wanted me to do things that made me face fears, so I took skydiving lessons and got my skydiving license. My first boyfriend loved to eat ethnic foods, so I developed an interest in those foods. My second boyfriend wanted to live in Japan, so I followed him to Japan. It became a way of life to just be, go to, and do whatever anyone else wanted, never going against their flow. I readily allowed everyone else's desires to become my own. In the process, I was losing my authentic self and not realizing that I was becoming increasingly unhappy because of it.

After so many years of pretending to myself that I was being myself, I actually thought I was just an unhappy person. The phrase, "Just be yourself" went right over my head. I kept myself busy being what other people wanted me to be and doing what was expected of me so I could be loved and accepted. I was afraid to have an opinion, speak up, or go against the status quo. Secretly, I was unhappy and depressed and didn't know that not being true to me was one of the many reasons for my unhappiness.

I was living the life of someone I was not, unaware that, deep down, I just wanted to be loved for who I really am. I lived this paradox daily. Only later did I realize the importance of living a life that is congruent with the person you are on the inside.

Your Authentic Self

So, how about you? Is your life more in tune with your authentic self (who you *really* are) or your "false" self (who others think you are or have said you are)?

When someone asks who you are, usually you answer with your name, profession, or social status. The answer could sound something like, "I'm Janice. I'm a mom and an office manager, and I live in Honolulu." What you answer is what we see on the outside and what others use to define you. That is not who you really are.

The true essence of who you are can be referred to as "your authentic self." This is the essence of the "real you" found at your absolute core, connected to your spirit and your heart. This part of you is not defined by your external trappings or by somebody else's rules and traditions. It is the synthesis of all your unique skills, talents, wisdom, desires, and characteristics. It cannot be defined, yet it needs to express in your life in its own way. Your authentic self is who you really are, rather than what you believe you are supposed to be and do.

Your False Self

When you are not living congruently with your authentic self, you are living the life of your false or fictional self, which is what I was doing. Living from your false self feels somehow incomplete, like living in a hole deep inside you. The more inauthentic and false you are, the bigger the hole feels, yet because it is easier to be who your family and friends expect you to be rather than who you want to be, you just keep plugging along. Living as your false self is a huge drain of energy.

Living a False Life

I have a long-time client named Avelina. I see her every year. She is a 44-year-old mother of two teenage daughters. She has always been a fulltime homemaker, raising the girls and taking care of the home while her husband amply provides them with all the comforts of life. Her family and friends envy her good fortune, yet she shares with me in confidence that she feels empty inside. She loves her daughters and her husband dearly, but her life is not the life she dreamed of; she feels she ended up with it by default.

Unlike some people in a similar situation, Avelina knows what she likes. The kind of metaphysical/spiritual work I do interests and excites her (although she has to keep our sessions secret from her husband), and she loves photography. She dreams of getting a job as a photographer's assistant and eventually becoming a photographer, but her family doesn't approve, especially her husband who is very traditional and doesn't see the need for her to work since he provides so well.

Anytime Avelina gets the courage to bring up her idea to her husband, he forbids it, the daughters side with him, and so she relents, feeling guilty for bringing it up and upsetting everyone. Afterwards, she talks herself into remembering her role as a mom and wife and moves further into inauthenticity. She returns to being a member of the club of the living dead. Year by year, I see her become more and more withdrawn and depressed.

Avelina thinks that getting a job is the issue and that if she gets a job, she will be happy. While a job would certainly help, the core issue is that she is living a false life, and her soul is crying out to live the way she wants to live. Like all of us, she has a deep inner longing to be loved for who she is, not for what she does.

The Good Old Days before We Were False

Do you remember when you were a child, before you knew what it was like to live falsely? Did you wake up in the summer full of joyful anticipation for the day? Remember when you could be with your friends and play and do and say whatever you wanted?

Ah! Those were the days, however short-lived. At some later point in our lives, we learned that we needed to do certain things in order to get along in this world, things like withholding our feelings and our opinions and doing the "right thing" according to those around us. We were told to listen to our teachers, keep a low profile, and even to lie about what we felt, saw, and heard.

Based on what other people say, we have slowly but surely planted within ourselves false beliefs, other people's opinions and judgments, self-criticisms, pain, anger, negative emotions, feelings of abandonment, and so on. These things fool us into thinking that we know who we are. However, when the need to be authentic outweighs the need to be who others say we are, we reach a tipping point and have to make changes.

Making a Break to Live Authentically

Antonio came to me after sixteen years of living up to the unreasonably high expectations of his wife and family. Not only were they controlling and hard to please, they were unwilling to let him "be himself." First, he fell into the role of pleasing his family and, later, his wife. Over time, like Avelina, he felt he was slowly but surely dying inside.

Antonio had wanted to break free for years, but his wife and his parents kept reminding him of his responsibility to keep the family together and make the marriage work. Given his wife and his family's outlook on divorce, he said it would actually be easier to commit suicide, so he stayed.

The day came, however, when he woke up and knew it was time to make a change, no matter what. He couldn't be who the others wanted him to be, anymore. As painful as the process was, he left his wife and later divorced her. Antonio's need to live an authentic life was, for him, a life-or-death issue.

How to Live Authentically

To live authentically, you have to be willing to go against what you have been conditioned to do if it doesn't match how you want to live. If you tend to be a people-pleaser, like Antonio, this is exceptionally difficult, especially if you have spent many years deferring to others or seeking outside validation.

The first step is to make a commitment to listening to your authentic voice, the voice of your intuition. It is the quiet "inner voice," not the louder, repetitious mind chatter that evokes anxiety and fear.

Antonio's authentic voice had been whispering to him all along that he needed to make a change, but his mind chatter constantly drowned it out: "The loss of respect and honor is too great," "The rejection is too painful," "The failure is too deep," etc. The tipping point came when his authentic voice got so loud that he couldn't deny the truth of it.

Your intuition will always tell you the most authentic choice for you, the choice that will be congruent with your life. Keep listening for it. When you hear it, always make a point of acknowledging it. Don't suppress it and don't judge it.

The Journey towards Authenticity

During certain periods of your life more than others, you will feel that you can no longer abide by specific unspoken agreements you have with those around you. Whenever you feel you are living a compromised existence, here are five steps you can take to start the journey towards living a more authentic life. It will be helpful to use a journal or notebook to record your thoughts.

Step One: Affirm and clarify what you do not want.

Begin by admitting what you *do not* want. Make a list that is as long as you like. Be honest. There is no right or wrong way to feel. Your list might look something like this:

- I don't want to be depended on to do *everything*.
- I don't want to be tied down to the extent that I am.
- I don't want to do what everyone else wants me to do.
- I don't want to feel lazy.

- I don't want to feel overwhelmed.
- I don't want to socialize with my old work friends, anymore.

Had I been honest with myself in college, I would have admitted that I didn't want to study biology and be a doctor, and I didn't really like everything that Jeff liked. Now, looking back, I see that it was a time when it was more important for me to please others and feel wanted than it was to please myself and be excluded.

Step Two: Know the difference between being inauthentic and authentic.

Everyone has "symptoms" in the form of feelings or behavior that tell them when they are being inauthentic and when they are being authentic. Become familiar with them so you can better gauge where you are in the various situations in your life.

Symptoms of being your false self

When your inner needs and values don't match your outer expression, you feel anxious, you want to people-please and impress others, and you agree to do things you later regret. You either hide your true feelings or deny them. You feel overwhelmed and even hopeless at times. Your mind chatters incessantly, and you have to rationalize your decisions. You feel depressed. You feel resentful or angry with certain people and situations. You feel empty inside.

Symptoms of being your authentic self

When your inner needs match your outer expression, you feel optimistic and are able to be honest and open. You go with the flow and are open to change. You listen to your feelings, take responsibility when appropriate, make healthy choices, and know how to ask for help. You also have no problem accepting and receiving. When you commit to someone or something, you feel good and don't have any problem saying No when something doesn't fit into your schedule or your plans. You feel happy a lot of the time.

Step Three: Make a list of situations in which you are being inauthentic.

Using your awareness of symptoms as a guide, look at your life and determine with whom and in what situations you tend to be your false self. Make a list. Be honest. Do not succumb to rationalizing and excusing things from this list.

Go through your list and ask yourself the following questions about each situation or person:

- What is the thought or belief I have about myself that causes me to be false?

- Does holding onto this belief or attitude make me feel happy?
- Do I get more of what I want by holding onto to this?
- If not, does it keep me locked into circumstances that I don't want?

Asking yourself questions brings hidden patterns of thought to the surface, and these bring new awareness. When we peel back the layers of what is false, we can more easily see what is true. Asking yourself questions is the key.

So, for example, if Avelina were to do this step, her journal entry would look something like this:

I am my false self with my husband and daughters. What causes me to be false is the belief that it is a woman's duty to obey her husband and be a "good" wife, and the belief that putting your own needs before the needs of your family is "wrong." Holding onto these beliefs does not make me happy, and I get less of what I want by holding onto them. These beliefs keep me in circumstances that I don't want.

Step Four: Write actionable, accountable steps you can take towards authenticity.

Once you are aware of when or with whom your false self shows up and can see the belief that is connected to it, you have a starting point from which to plan a course of action.

- In each situation or with each person you see that you are your false self and *are ready to make a change*, write down three steps you can take immediately that will lead you closer to your authentic self.
- Next to each action step, write down the date by which you will do it. Put it in your calendar and write it on any to-do lists you have.
- If you have a close friend you can trust to be your accountability partner, tell him or her what you have committed to and why, and ask that person to check back with you on a specific date.

Avelina may not be ready to work on the "big one" (her husband and family), but she may be ready to let go of some social obligations she no longer enjoys, or she may be ready to set new rules with the neighbor who visits without an invitation. Working on the smaller things will raise her "vibrating point" (see the Law of Vibration in Chapter Four) so that, in the future, she will be more ready to address the bigger issues. See where you are ready to start moving towards authenticity. Every step counts; in fact, your happiness depends on it.

Step Five: What are the benefits of taking these steps for everyone who will be affected?

As you write your action steps towards authenticity, you inevitably will feel pangs of guilt and even fear as you imagine the reaction of those affected by the actions you plan. You may feel that you are being selfish, and your mind may try to convince you to keep things as they are and not rock the boat. You may feel bad that someone else might have to be inconvenienced or that you will cause them to get upset. These are all very normal reactions.

To help neutralize the emotional charge and mental chatter, get centered prior to taking action. One way to do this is to write down all the ways that you and anyone else who will be affected by this action will benefit. The more clearly you can see that the benefits of your action are equal to the challenges it will bring, the easier it will be to proceed.

If you want to take this one step further, write down the worst things you think could happen if you take these steps and decide how you would handle them. Sometimes, once we define the fears that are holding us back and bring them out into the open, they are not as terrible as we think.

How Living Authentically Benefits All

Let's say that you have lost the joy in being the team mom for your child's soccer team. You have done it for three years now, and they expect you to continue. The first year it was fun, the second year you realized it was "not for you," and when they asked you for the third year, you wanted to say No but you "couldn't." You feel guilty for wanting to say No for the fourth year, and worse, you feel you don't have a good reason not to do it.

First of all, you *do* have a good reason: You want to be authentic, and you don't feel like doing it. Write down the benefits that you and everyone will experience if you say No. The more benefits you find, the easier and more natural it will be to turn down the fourth year.

Here's an example of what some benefits might be:

Benefits to You

You will feel better, have more time to do the project you've been putting off, have time to cook healthier meals for your family, be able to feel more productive at work since you won't have to leave early, and will feel better about yourself.

Benefits to Others

Someone else will have the opportunity to step up, and someone else may be happier to do it than you are. This will bring a better energy to the team. Also, when you do see your family, you will be more present with them, your children will get more of your attention, and you will set a good example.

Take it Step by Step

The longer you have been inauthentic, the longer and slower the journey will be, back to your authentic self. It's easy to get caught up in a fantasy that, once you are being authentic in one area, you will be confident, balanced, and centered *all* the time. However, as you can already imagine, some situations are harder to deal with and may cause us to regress into old patterns. Take it slow. Awareness is the first step.

As you go through each day, begin to notice with which people you feel more yourself—more authentic—and with which people you feel less so. It is always a good sign when you feel expanded and relaxed. When you feel limited or contracted, take it as a sign that you are not being present and authentic.

Simple Ways to Bring in Authenticity

Here are a few of my favorite ways to get that expanded-and-relaxed authentic feeling if you are missing it.

- **Be gentle with yourself.** Sometimes we expect a lot of ourselves. We set impossible standards and then beat ourselves up for not doing what we set out to do. Remember to be gentle with yourself and praise yourself for what you *do* do.
- **Recognize your uniqueness.** We can get so caught up in trying to fit in that we forget we each have our individual talents and skills. Really appreciate what makes you special and unique. No one else is like you, and *that* is what makes you special!
- **Enjoy key moments.** Life brings us a series of moments, some more memorable than others. Remember to stop occasionally and enjoy the moment you are in.
- **Look for new options.** Trying to choose between two options can make you feel stuck. Instead, create a third option to explore and this will move you towards more possibilities.
- **Support something you believe in.** Suppressing anything drains energy. If there is something you feel strongly about, support it—in person, online, or by phone. This will help you feel expanded and real.

Don't feel you have to make sweeping changes in your life all at once in order to be authentic and more present with your life. Anything you do, no matter how small, can shift how you experience your life immediately. Making a choice to live your life authentically is a lifelong journey.

Key Points

- Your "authentic self" is who you really are and your "false self" is who others think you are or what you believe you are supposed to be or do.
- Your authentic self—the spirit of the "real you" found at your core—is the synthesis of all your values, unique skills, talents, wisdom, desires, and uniqueness, and it needs expression in your life.
- Based on what other people say, we have slowly but surely planted within ourselves false beliefs, other people's opinions and judgments, self-criticisms, and negative emotions that fool us into thinking we know who we are.
- When you are living life as your false self, you feel like you are living in a hole deep inside you.
- You will make changes when the need to be who you really are outweighs the need to be who others say you are.
- Living authentically means you have to be willing to go against what you have been conditioned to do if it doesn't match who you are.
- Listen to your authentic inner voice. It will always tell you the most authentic choice for you, the choice that will be congruent with your life.
- Take steps towards authenticity when you are ready:

  - Admit and list what you do not want.
  - Know the symptoms of being authentic and inauthentic.
  - Make a list of situations in which you are being inauthentic.
  - Write actionable, accountable steps you can take towards authenticity.
  - Write down all the ways that you and anyone else who will be affected by this action will benefit.

- Awareness is key. Begin to notice the people with whom you feel authentic. Feeling expanded and relaxed is always a good sign. When you feel limited or contracted, take it as a sign that you are not being present and authentic.
- Simple ways to bring in authenticity:

- – Be gentle with yourself.
- – Recognize your uniqueness.
- – Remember to stop occasionally and enjoy the moment you are in.
- – When you feel stuck between two options, look for a third option to open up possibilities.
- – Support something you believe in.

- Don't feel you have to make sweeping changes in your life all at once. A first step is all it takes.

TEN

DON'T ALLOW EVERY DRIVER INTO YOUR LANE

Happiness comes from saying both Yes and No.

If you say Yes to every driver who wants to enter your lane, you will be the last person to reach your destination, if you ever do. Conversely, if you say No to every request, you will be wherever you are alone. Traffic flows most smoothly when there is an easy give-and-take among drivers.

Humorist Josh Billings really struck a chord with his audience when he said, "Half of the troubles of your life can be traced to saying yes too quickly and not saying no soon enough." Everyone in the audience was laughing out loud because it rings true for all of us, doesn't it?

Haven't we all said Yes when we really wanted to say No? Or said No when we really wanted to say Yes?

When a friend asks, "Can you help me with my garage sale this weekend?" and you say, "I'll be there!" do you immediately think, "Argh! Why did I agree?" And when someone asks, "Can I give you a hand with that?" and you say, "No, thank you! I can manage," do you wish you had said, "Yes, thank you. I could really use some help?"

Why don't we automatically say what we want? Mostly, it's because we're uncomfortable about being authentic, we worry about what other people think, and our upbringing, culture, or subconscious beliefs get in the way. Yet, much of this can be overcome with awareness, preparation, and a strategy.

What is more challenging for you: not being able to say No, or not being able to say Yes?

Saying No When You Mean Yes

If you are saying No when you really mean Yes, you may be blocking what you really want in your life, which is a little more support. Being able to receive is just as important as being able to give.

Joanie is an example. Joanie felt unsupported by her husband and was beginning to resent him because of it. Those who know her describe her as an overachiever. She is productive, talented, successful, and accomplished. Pondering this, I wondered which was the case: Was her husband *choosing* not to support her, or was she *not letting* him support her? I questioned Joanie in detail, and she realized that every time her husband offered to do something for her, like carry in the groceries, pay the bills, fill her car up with gas, or fix a gadget, she would refuse and say that she had it handled.

Why would she refuse even when she really wanted help and then complain and be resentful because she wasn't getting any?

It's because Joanie had a belief that she *should* be able to do everything herself. If she didn't do it all, she felt she would be considered incompetent. She had been resenting her husband for not carrying more of the load and thinking that he should insist. In reality, she was calling the shots and forcing herself to be Superwoman.

How to Get Past Saying No When You Mean Yes

To get to Yes, Joanie had to do several things:

- Accept responsibility for the current state of affairs (see Chapter One).
- Accept that her husband *wanted* to support her but was responding to what she was saying. He couldn't read her mind, and so, when she said she had something handled, he trusted that.
- Accept that if she wants her husband's support, she has to be open to receiving it, otherwise it will never happen.
- Reframe her belief about competency. No one else thinks she is less competent if she receives support. It's all in her head, and it's up to her to change.

Joanie worked on these things. Now, when her husband offers to help, she accepts more often than before, and it has improved their relationship. All the while she was blaming her husband, she didn't realize she was blocking the support she desired. (See the Law of Compensation in Chapter Four.)

Start Saying Yes and Receive What You Want

If you tend to block help and support when they are offered, here are three easy steps you can take immediately to change your pattern:

- Be aware. Catch yourself in the moment. At first, you may catch yourself too late because past behavior has conditioned you to say No when help is offered; keep at it, however, and soon you'll be able to respond with a more authentic answer.
- Check in with your body. Just as you are about to say No when you really want to say Yes, how do you feel? If you think about saying No, does your breath become shallow, your body tense? Does your mind start rationalizing why you need to turn down help? Whenever you are internally incongruent, your body will react with tension and your mind with chatter. These are symptoms of not being authentic (Chapter Nine).
- Rehearse your desired response. At night, take a few moments to go over the day and find times you said No when you wanted to say Yes. Visualize how it would feel if you had said Yes, and what the result would have been. If you wanted help and didn't ask for it, create a positive vision of what would have happened if you had asked.
- Follow the above steps and you will notice a shift in your ability to say Yes and greater ease in asking for help. Saying Yes when you want to say Yes is congruent and authentic.

Saying Yes When You Mean No

Here are four of the most common reasons for saying Yes when you mean No. Interestingly, each of these reasons correlates to either the physical, emotional, mental, or spiritual body (Chapter Four):

Reason Number One Relates to the Physical: *This will take no time at all.*

Have you ever had a block of time and a list of things to do, but those things never got physically done even though you thought you had enough time? Unrealistic expectations frustrate us when we don't get things done. In addition, we give our valuable time away by saying Yes to others even though we don't really have enough time to do what we need to do for ourselves.

A simple solution will help you understand the time it takes to do things. Break down what you have to do into smaller, mini tasks. For example, something that used to be on my to-do list every month was: "Prepare books for distributor." At only four words, it looks like a fast task. Actually, it takes 50 minutes!

- Unpack a hundred books from storage: 10 minutes
- Put on award stickers: 10 minutes
- Repackage into four boxes of 25: 10 minutes
- Prepare and print packing slip: 5 minutes
- Put in pouch and seal onto boxes: 5 minutes
- Take empty cardboard boxes to recycling bin: 10 minutes

Almost all the items on my to-do list were tasks that took longer than I thought. When broken down, all of them took over thirty minutes. It's no wonder I could never finish everything in the allotted time! Being realistic about how much time my tasks took gave me a better handle on how much time I really had. It further helped me to prioritize and delegate low-priority items (like preparing books for the distributor) so I could spend more time on things I really wanted to do (like write books)!

When you have a clear handle on what time really means, as well as the time you need to do what you need to do, you will have a clearer idea about when you can say Yes and when you need to say No confidently—because you literally don't have the physical time.

Reason Number Two Relates to the Emotional: *It feels good to be liked.*

Wanting to be liked isn't a bad thing, but when we make our own value and worth dependent on what others think, then we've set up a no-win scenario. Why? Because it means that we live by a "rule" that says, "If you take care of yourself, you disappoint someone else." It's a subtle rule that many of us have in place. When you depend on others to define your worth, it is easy to feel worthless unless you are "proving" your value to others by saying Yes.

The only way around this dilemma is to focus on finding the value in who you are. Find the abundance in you by working with the Law of Abundance (Chapter Four). Take time to connect to your spiritual self (Chapter Seven) and understand your true, expanded nature and the value of who you are.

Reason Number Three Relates to the Mental: *Everything and everyone is important.*

If only everyone's request for your time was in line with the top priorities in your life, things would be so much easier. Since life doesn't work that way, it is up to you to determine what is important enough to say Yes to, and what isn't.

Priorities change over time. You have certain priorities when you are building your career. These change when you become a parent, go through an illness, or when you retire. If you don't identify your present priorities and values, you will say Yes without realizing that what you agreed to is not in line with your highest values and with those people who are priorities in your life—including you.

For example, you may love your friends and feel they are a priority, however, are they a greater priority than your partner and children? Are they more important than your work? How about you? Are they a greater priority than you? There is no right or wrong answer, only what is right for you.

Once you know your current highest priority, here is something you can ask yourself when a request or favor comes in: "If I say Yes, is it directly related to my top priorities?" or "If I say Yes, will it take me away from my top priorities and what I most value?" When you make a choice that honors your priorities, you might feel a twinge of guilt. In the long run, though, you will feel better when you honor what is important to you—not necessarily what is important to others.

Reason Number Four Relates to the Spiritual: *I love helping everyone out.*

Doing things for others models spiritual generosity. Extending help to those around us when they need our support is something that makes us feel good in our hearts. An equal exchange of giving and receiving is healthy, necessary, and a part of being human. However, when your giving role in certain relationships becomes routine and "expected," or your giving stops being a "good thing" for the other person, causing them to be dependent and lazy, it may be a good time to reevaluate your actions.

We can easily get stuck into doing something for others that they can do for themselves. As your priorities shift, reconsider what you are presently doing and whether it is an act of giving that is positive and healthy, or whether it is time to let others take responsibility for what they need. When we do things for others that they *can* do for themselves, we deprive them of the opportunity to grow.

Overstretching yourself at the cost of yourself and others is a lose-lose situation.

Other Reasons for Saying Yes When You Want to Say No

You may resonate with some of the other reasons listed below.

You want to be agreeable. You don't want to alienate yourself or cause problems, so you conform to the requests of others.

- *You want to avoid conflict.* You are afraid the other person will be angry if you say No, or that you will have to involve yourself in some other kind of unpleasant confrontation.

- *You feel that you will lose an opportunity.* You worry that if you say No, you will miss out on future possibilities that this opportunity might bring your way.
- *You want to maintain the relationship.* If you say No, you fear that the other person might feel rejected and that the incident will change the nature of your relationship.
- *You feel that your time is not valuable and that you should give it up to someone who needs it more.* You figure that you don't have anything planned, anyway, and the other person really needs help, so why not?

Mental Misconceptions

Many of these reasons are misconceptions that your mind has led you to believe are true. Is it true that saying No means you are rude or disagreeable? Saying No does not always lead to conflict, and you will definitely not lose opportunities by saying No. Your time is yours to spend the way you want. No one has a claim over your time unless you allow it. These are all false beliefs that your mind has perpetuated.

It's Never Too Late

I received a letter from a woman asking my advice. She was unhappy with her life, and she was sure that it stemmed from her inability to say No. She reported that she felt like a doormat and was losing control of her time and her life. People were always asking her to do things for them, and she felt bad if she said No. Yet, she was tired of doing things for others and nothing for herself. She wanted to make changes, but she felt guilty and had no idea how to start. She wondered if this type of thing shows up in an astrological chart and asked whether some people were destined to be pushovers. She signed her letter "Save Me" and said that she would appreciate suggestions on how to say No.

It is never too late to take back the reins of your life. She was not destined to be this way forever, and especially not if she chose to put forth the effort to evolve towards living an empowered life.

Astrologically, although certain combinations of planetary energies cause one person to be more altruistic than another, our charts do not determine our destiny. We always have the choice to consciously evolve and change things in our lives. Saying No is more difficult for some people, but you can learn this skill if you are committed to getting on the No train. If you don't value your time and energy, no one else will—as "Save Me" was seeing.

Change will not happen overnight, but if you start working on it, you can develop a new skill and "language" that will begin to serve you in a new way. I suggested that she connect with someone on this, either a trusted friend or a professional, someone who not only would hold her accountable but also would support her as she celebrates her No successes.

I have firsthand experience with this, and I completely understand how the letter writer felt. It took me some time to understand why I couldn't say No and to find the courage to do so.

Different Ways to Say No

Learn different ways to say No. Visualize yourself doing it, and then once you actually start *saying* it, you will realize that it is not as hard as you thought. The best thing is that you will not only reclaim time for yourself, but you will also feel a new sense of empowerment. Saying No is just making a choice each time you are confronted with that choice. When you begin to respect your time, others will, too.

In the future, use one of the following responses, the one that best fits your situation, or create your own.

If you are too busy:

Rosa, I'm happy you felt comfortable enough to ask me, but there are so many things going on in my life that I am just not able to commit to anything right now. I'm already overextended.

This is a great way to let the requester know that your plate is full. If it is appropriate, share what is going on to give an idea of why you are turning down the request.

If they know your life well and you can't use the "I'm too busy" excuse:

Rick, there are so many things I've been wanting to do that I haven't done, and I'm tired of making excuses. Last week, I made a commitment to start. I'm really sorry, but I will be tied up for the next few weeks.

When a few weeks have passed, you can maintain that you don't have the time.

If you get a last-minute request:

Darn, Katie! I am literally in the middle of some things that I need to complete. I hope you can find someone to help you. If not, I might be able to help you out next week.

If you are in the middle of something, the above wording is perfect. Have it ready, even if you are not in the middle of something and just want the time for yourself. You are never under any obligation. Your time is yours, and you always have a choice as to how much you give away and when. If you really wouldn't mind helping out the person later, mention another time that works for you.

If you are tied up with other things:

That sounds great, but I'm going to have to say No.

Acknowledge that the request or suggestion is wonderful, however tell the other that you are tied up with projects right now or that you are taking time off from social engagements this week to catch up on some personal commitments or that you have a prior engagement, etc.

If you want to buy yourself time:

Let me think about it (or check my schedule) and get back to you.

This buys you time when you think you are interested but are not ready to say Yes. If you are the type to jump in and later regret it, memorize it. Sometimes, people ask you to do things that sound great in the moment, and you agree only to discover later that you wished you hadn't said Yes. Commit this to memory and make it a habit.

However, if you really are not interested, don't lead the person on. Use one of the other immediate No responses.

If someone is pitching you something you want to turn down:

What you are describing sounds great, but it really doesn't meet my current needs (or doesn't work in light of what is going on in my life). Thank you for sharing, however. I will be sure to keep it in mind.

If you do not resonate with what another person is pitching, it is better to say No right in the beginning. For example, many people who are involved in network marketing or multilevel marketing want to share with others the value they have found in it. Saying No early on prevents you from spending time and energy on something that can drag on longer than you want it to.

If you just have to say No:

Thank you for asking but…I can't. If I can think of anyone who can help you, I'll let you know.

There are times when you just have to say No, short and sweet, and you can build up too many barriers in your mind to saying it. Try it for simple requests. Once you say it, you'll be surprised at how much nicer the response is than you had imagined it would be—and how much better you will feel.

Find Time for Yourself—Now

Do you need more free time than you have? Look through your social calendar and daily calendar to see where you can free up some time. Make a list of anything you see there that you wish you hadn't committed to. Add to that list anything you are currently doing that you would like to let go of.

Next, for each commitment that you want to let go of, make two lists: one list of the personal benefits you will reap by saying No to these commitments and one list of the benefits that the other person may potentially experience if you say No.

By taking the time to write out a list of the benefits and advantages of saying No, you will be better able to hold your boundaries and not feel guilty.

Give yourself permission

To let go of a commitment and free up some time, give yourself permission to say something like this: *Joelle, something has come up for me, and I won't be able to make it. Thank you so much for the invitation. Maybe we can reschedule this later.* If the event you will be missing is a group event, add: *My thoughts will be with everyone, and I am sure you will all have a great time.*

Once you create the habit of always considering both sides of a situation and seeing that saying No has benefits for both you and the other person, you will feel more empowered to speak your truth.

Still Can't Say No? Say Yes! (Then No)

If you feel uncomfortable when you envision using some variation of the responses above, maybe a different technique is in order. The Yes/No strategy may resonate with your style and personality better. Sometimes, the way you say No is more important than the fact that you are saying No.

Jacinta: *There's an art event downtown tonight, and I have no one to go with. Will you come with me?*

You: *Yes! I'd love to, but unfortunately, I have a project I have to focus on tonight.*

Bob: *Can you make it to the meeting this afternoon? I just want to get your feedback.*

You: *Yes! I'd love to, but I have another meeting I need to attend.*

Wendy: *We're doing a car wash fundraiser for my son's baseball team. Can you help?*

You: *Yes! Under normal circumstances, I would be delighted to, but I promised Bill I'd help him clear out the garage.*

Phone Caller: *Hello! Would you have a few minutes to complete our survey?*

You: *Yes, I enjoy doing surveys, but you've caught me at an inconvenient time. Please accept my apology.*

Keep a Balanced Perspective and Honor Yourself

In every situation, saying No and saying Yes have equal benefits and drawbacks. Look at all situations with a balanced perspective so that you can make the right decision for you, not for the other person. Sometimes, all you need is just a bit of strategy and preparation, and you can use some of the suggestions in this chapter to help. When in doubt, ask yourself, "I *can* do it, but do I *want* to?" Listen to that authentic voice deep inside you and honor yourself.

Key Points

- We don't say what we want mostly because we feel uncomfortable about being authentic and worry about what other people think.
- If you say No when you really mean Yes, you may be blocking support that you want.
- Receiving is as important as giving. Three steps for opening up to receive support:

  - Be aware and catch yourself just as you are about to say No.
  - Check in with your body and see how you feel.
  - If during the day you said No when you wanted to say Yes, rehearse your desired response at the end of the day.
  - You are never under any obligation to say Yes. Your time is yours, and you always have a choice as to how much you give away and when.

- The reasons we say Yes when we want to say No correlate to our four bodies:

  - Physical: *This will take no time at all.* We don't realize how much physical time it takes to actually do things.
  - Emotional: *It feels good to be liked.* We depend on others to define our worth, so we do things for approval.
  - Mental: *Everything and everyone is important.* We have not defined our personal priorities.
  - Spiritual: *I love helping everyone out.* We do things for others that they can do for themselves and deprive them of taking responsibility.

- Other reasons you may resist saying No:
  - You want to be agreeable.
  - You want to avoid conflict.
  - You feel you will lose an opportunity.
  - You want to maintain the relationship.
  - You feel your time is not valuable and you should give it up to someone who needs it.

- Learn to say No if you are too busy, get a last-minute request, are tied up with things, need to buy yourself time, want to turn down a pitch, or just have to say a simple No.
- Find time for yourself by looking in your calendar and bowing out of events you would like to let go of.
- If it is too hard to say No right off, try the Yes/No strategy. Sometimes, the way you say No is more important than the fact that you are saying it.

ELEVEN

TAKE CARE OF YOUR VEHICLE

....

There's more to your body than meets the eye.

....

Timely maintenance of your vehicle helps you get on down the road without unnecessary crisis. Check your brakes often and they are less likely to fail when you need them. Get regular tune-ups to pinpoint problems before they become extra costly. Notice unusual noises and have them checked out. Get your exterior and interior detailed to prevent rust and enjoy feeling better about your car because it looks shiny and well kept.

Now, how do you feel about your body? Do you love, or at least like, how you look? Is your health what you want it to be? Are you sleeping well? I heard a phrase years ago that has stuck with me: "If you don't take care of your body, where are you going to live?" It's true, yet I know firsthand that taking care of your body is not as easy as just wanting to exercise or eat a healthy diet.

Although you may intend to take care of your body, your mental thoughts, emotional state, spiritual lessons, and even planetary cycles can come into play. All of these affect your experience of your physical body.

The Void of Unhappiness

Remember the story I told in Chapter Nine about losing my identity and not living authentically because I was copying others and doing what everyone else wanted me to do? Well, the further away from my authentic self I got, the unhappier I became. What I didn't share earlier is that I began emotionally eating to fill the inner void I felt because I was not being authentic.

The more I ate, the unhappier I felt, and the bigger I got. I gained over thirty pounds in just a few years by eating pizza, ice cream, junk food, and fast food. Being a size 13/14 created even more emotional stress for me, because not only did I hate being an insecure, inauthentic, unhappy people-pleaser, I also hated the acne, the excess fat, and the way they both made me look and feel.

I was uninspired, unhealthy, and lazy. I was so lazy that I skipped classes just because I didn't want to walk up the steep hill to my dorm room afterwards. Eventually, I realized that I had to go to class, so I creatively devised a technique to forge parking passes that looked so real I fooled the parking attendants for almost a year. With these special-access parking passes, I could park near my dorm room and drive to class to avoid walking up the hill.

Had I just made the passes for myself, all would have been well. However, my desire to be liked and accepted led me to make these coveted passes for anyone who wanted one (I didn't know how to say No back then). Just a month before graduation, though, I got caught. I was arrested by campus police for being a "ring leader." I was taken to jail, photographed, fingerprinted, and charged with forgery. In addition, I was told I would be kicked out of school and would not be able to graduate.

Fortunately, a lawyer got me off on probation because it was a first-time offense, and the university made a decision to excuse me since one of the students who used my forged parking pass was the son of a university official. Thankfully, because of this connection, I was able to stay in school and graduate.

Looking Good Alone Won't Fill the Void

Since then, I have become active and fit, lost more than thirty pounds, and shed the acne. Even so, there is a part of me that still feels like "Fat Al, the Pillsbury Dough Girl," the nickname my dorm mates gave me when I was pale and chubby. During those emotionally challenging years, I dreamed of being thin and beautiful. I fantasized that if I were physically "perfect," my life would be, too. In my vision of myself, I was popular and filled with confidence. In this vision I had appealing nicknames, nice friends, and the guys I liked, liked me back. I thought if I looked good, I would be happy.

After I graduated from college, I painstakingly began the process of taking more responsibility for my life physically, emotionally, and mentally. Over time,

I slowly lost the weight and reshaped my appearance, but these things didn't bring me the "perfect" life I was dreaming of. I was still an insecure, inauthentic, unhappy people-pleaser—I just didn't have the extra weight and the acne to go along with it.

From this period of my life, I learned that how people actually look and what they think and feel about themselves exist as two separate issues. Unless we work on what we think about ourselves, we will never change the way people respond to us.

Accept How You Look, Mentally and Emotionally

Let's start with *not liking how you look* if that is where you are at. If you want to treat your body well, you've got to like it; or at least you have to stop wishing it were something other than what it is. In other words, you've got to first accept it. No matter what shape your body is in or how you think you look or wish you looked, you look that way for a purpose. The reality is, you look exactly the way you need to look in order to experience what you need to experience.

Are you ready to change the view you have of your body? If you have an overly active inner critic whose constant mental chatter highlights your physical shortcomings while ignoring your pleasing attributes, it's time to take control and talk back.

I have been on both sides of the fence, and whether I actually *was* fat or skinny, or *thought* I was fat or skinny, life was still challenging. Although how you look does have some impact on how people react to you, beauty is in the eye of the beholder, and the feeling of "beautiful" exists only in the mind of the beheld. In other words, it's ultimately what *you* say to yourself and what *you* think that matters.

What about a Makeover?

It is natural to want to look better. Makeovers in the form of new clothes, plastic surgery, hair restoration, weight loss, or manicures all can be positive and uplifting, however only if you have the right attitude and do it for the right reason. Do you think it's time for you to get a makeover? (Men, this means you, too). If so, here are some things to review before you make that appointment:

- A makeover won't do anything for you if you do it to match someone else's definition of beauty. It will help if it brings you closer to *your* definition of beauty.
- Anything you do will be a waste of time and money if don't like yourself. If you hate yourself, you'll find something to hate about what you just had done.

- Accept that you will always look like you. If you put a wig and lipstick on a goat, you won't get a supermodel; you'll just get a hairy-headed goat with red lips.
- Don't expect that a makeover will get you the mate or the job you want. You might feel more confident, but looking "better" won't bring into your life anything more than you already have.

Makeovers are great boosters, not because you will look better (though it's likely you may), but because you will *believe* that you look better. That is the magic and the power of the mind. If *you* think you look better, even if others don't, you will have more confidence. When I was a member of an exercise club, one woman I met told me how much more confident she felt after her lip-plumping (it sounded more like "whip-pumping") and her Botox treatments as she struggled to wink.

I also remember seeing a formerly bald older gentleman who got a full head of black hair. In my opinion, the youthful black hair did not quite "match" the age spots and sagging skin of a man in his late seventies, but he told me with a huge smile that he never felt better—and really, that's all that really matters.

However, even if a physical change isn't noticeable to others it can have a big impact on transforming a person's view of themselves. I remember seeing one client that I hadn't seen for a while and thought she looked great – though I couldn't put my finger on anything specific about her appearance that was new. She shared with me that she had a procedure done to remove some discoloration on her jaw line (which I had never noticed before) and that she felt so much more confident and upbeat about herself.

Inner Transformation and How You See Yourself

To make any outer change last, there must be a corresponding change in how you see yourself. If you are the type who always has something positive to say about yourself and how you look, you can skip to the next section. Okay, now that one person has moved on, I hope the rest of you find the following useful:

- **Change what you say:** People who know and love you see your positive attributes and have gotten over whatever shortcomings you may have. Start looking for something about yourself to praise. You don't even have to believe what you are saying. I know it is hard, but you just have to do it. Self-talk is subtle, yet profound; it has an effect on your energetic presence and how others perceive you.
- **Change whom you compare yourself to:** Once you have found some positive things to put your attention on, stop comparing yourself to the

people you see on television and in magazines. They make up only a miniscule percentage of the population. If you are going to make comparisons based on any rational sense, compare yourself to the people in line at the supermarket: that would be realistic.

- **Be open with someone you trust:** If you have a deep issue about accepting how you look, find someone to share this with—from your heart. At its core, the longing to be beautiful is a longing to be free from shame. Whether comments from childhood have left you feeling less than beautiful or you are suffering from self-judgments based on the public's idea of beauty, open up and share how you really feel about how you look. Doing this won't change your looks, but you'll feel much freer if you allow another person to enter into the reality of your experience.

As you implement one or more of the above options, you will begin the process of slowly transforming your "inner" view of yourself to a view that is more balanced. Always keep in the back of your mind that being unapologetically yourself will make you more attractive than ever, and it *will* eventually bring you everything you once thought beauty would bring—acceptance, power, meaningful friendships, self-esteem, intimacy—and yes, even happiness!

Sleep and Stress

On another note, how are you sleeping at night? Are you getting enough sleep? When I was growing up, the adults were constantly telling me, "Go to bed early! Get your beauty sleep!" I thought it was just a phrase until I grew up and understood that sleep really is related to beauty.

As you know, when you sleep well, you not only feel better, but you also think better and look better. Unfortunately, studies show that stress affects the quality of our sleep. The more stress you have, the more challenging it is to sleep well. The less you sleep, the more stress hormones are pumped out by the adrenal glands. This is certainly a Catch 22.

"New" stressors and changing sleep patterns

We are in a time, thanks to technology, where life feels as though it's speeding up, making us feel we need to go faster and do more. We pile more on our plates get caught up in *doing* rather than *being*. I have noticed a "new" type of stress that has been steadily emerging and is adding to the day-to-day stress of jobs, family dynamics, and relationships. I am referring to the "stress" of needing to find our purpose, our reason for existence, our balance, and our happiness. And it is harder than ever to do so because there is so much to take us away from our center.

Can this new stress be responsible for your changing sleep patterns or quality of sleep? I remember times in the old days when I closed my eyes at night and did not wake up until the morning. However, as I started to "wake up" to wanting more purpose in my life, my sleep patterns started changing, and I was no longer able to sleep through the night.

In 2008 when I wrote my first book, *A Loving Guide to These Shifting Times,* I had been teaching spiritual workshops monthly all over the world for a few years. During that time, I found that 80-90 percent of the people who attended my presentations were also noticing changes in their sleep patterns. They were waking up sometime between two and four in the morning for no reason. (Three a.m. seemed to be a popular time.) Like me, they were not sleeping as soundly as before.

Planetary cycles prompt us to "wake up"

As an astrologer, I study planetary cycles that influence our personal lives and our collective evolution and growth. Astrological cycles have been prompting us to "wake up" to our lives in a new way. Many who "feel" it and want to reach a greater level of consciousness have similar symptoms, one of which is not sleeping as soundly as before.

When we are in rhythm with our daily life and purpose, as well as with the universe and planetary movements, sleep is deep and effortless. When we are not sleeping well, it is because there is something we need to wake up to. This could be anything from the need to let go of old patterns of thought and feeling about our physical bodies, to reassessing our purpose and what we want in our lives. At this time on our planet, we are being called to live more from our hearts than from our minds, and changing sleep patterns is one indication that we are waking up to that.

Now and continuing into 2016 and beyond, we are experiencing rare planetary cycles whose themes directly affect key areas of our lives. Planetary cycles bring awareness and initiate change. When change happens, we open up to new perspectives, we shift our thinking, and as a result, we evolve and grow.

One of the main planetary cycles involves Uranus (Mr. "I need freedom and change") and Pluto (Mr. "I need to transform and let go of the old"). The interaction of the two planets prompts us to look at how we are living. They are nudging us to reassess our patterns, our beliefs, our past choices, and our current actions. If we ignore their nudging and suppress change that is needed, stress and disturbed sleep will rule our lives.

Uranus and Pluto on a personal level

These two planets, Uranus and Pluto, are considered planetary "tough guys" in the astrological world, and their interaction is helping us to wipe away the old and bring in the new. If there is a need for reform in your life, Pluto will help to break down structures you have built that don't serve you anymore, and Uranus will help you to break out of old patterns and find personal freedom from limits you have created and lived by without questioning. The final gift of this cycle of planetary interaction is regeneration and much needed renewal, especially if you have wanted change in your life for some time now.

If you already have had major shifts in your life, these cycles will help you evolve further along your path. Continue to stay open to new awareness and further evolution. This will make it easier for you to help others understand what is going on when they come to you with stories of change.

Symptoms of Opening up to New Consciousness

During these times when strong planetary energies are creating opportunities for shifts in our lives, those of us who are opening up to our "inner selves" and a new consciousness seem to be collectively experiencing similar experiences. Do you have any of the following physical "symptoms"?

- **Triad Sleep Patterns:** Whereas from about 2000-2010 a majority of people mentioned regularly waking up between two and four a.m., the pattern has shifted again. Many people are unable to sleep continuously through the night. They sleep for a few hours, wake up, go back to sleep for a few hours, and wake up again. It's been referred to as a triad sleep pattern.
- **Vivid Dreams:** More people are having dreams that are vivid and feel "real." When we sleep, we not only recharge our physical bodies, we also connect more fully to the field of energy that keeps us in constant communication with our soul and spirit. Sleeping gives us the opportunity to connect more deeply with information from our higher consciousness, and vivid dreams are one of many signs of waking up to being more connected.

If you don't remember anything, it doesn't mean that you're not connecting to the field of energy; it simply means that remembering dreams is not one of your symptoms.

- **Weight Changes:** People are losing or gaining weight more than ever, and not just because of increased or reduced caloric intake or increased exercise. It goes beyond the physical. Those who are gaining weight have emotional issues that are coming to the surface to be dealt with (this is a good thing); those who are trying unsuccessfully to lose weight are in the process of working through internal "stuff," such as fears that have been holding them back. Those who have lost weight are processing their issues well and are "lightening" up emotionally, mentally, and physically.

- **A More Youthful Appearance:** Those who are actively working through their issues are looking light years younger! If this is you, it is a benefit of lightening your emotional load and changing your perspective on your life. If you can show a photo of yourself ten years ago and people say you look younger now, you are doing well. Keep going!

- **Unexplainable Physical Ailments:** Do you have body pains that show up "out of the blue" or nagging pains that just won't go away, many of which the doctors cannot find the origin of? Examine these more closely to see how they relate to past or present emotional or mental issues that you have not yet processed. According to my chiropractor, Dr. Chad Sato, when you suppress what you really want to say or do, your body may choose to express it in the form of pain or disease (*dis-ease*). Your emotions are playing a bigger part than ever by showing up in your overall health. It's not just physical, anymore.

- **Food Sensitivities:** Have you been more sensitive lately? Are there foods you used to love that no longer resonate with you? Some are noticing that, as they search for meaning and purpose, they crave healthier foods and don't eat as much meat or don't crave it in the same way as before. Vegetarianism and eating organic whole foods (versus processed) is on the rise, mostly for the health benefits and the "feel good" aspect they provide.

- **Addiction Awareness:** People who are "addicted" in some way are feeling it is time to get hold of their addictions and break the dependency. Any addictions you may have—sugar, excess alcohol, nicotine, excess caffeine, junk food—may be more noticeable than ever. The emotions behind these dependencies are calling to be processed.

"Secret" to Mastering the Physical

The secret to mastering your physical body is to realize that your physical well-being is connected to your emotional, mental, and spiritual well-being. Opening up to this realization will enable you to reach new levels in your life. From such a perspective, losing weight, for example, is no longer solely about counting calories and exercising; it becomes a matter of thinking "healthy," clearing out emotional clutter, and connecting to a higher source of consciousness.

Your physical body is the barometer by which you can measure your progress. Use it to your advantage: Listen to your intuition and feelings when you consider what to do, and change your thoughts about how you think you look. Remember at all times that you are part of a bigger picture. As you wake up to your purpose and experience more happiness, appreciate your body for what it does for you—ultimately, it keeps your heart beating and gives your spirit a place to live!

Key Points

- If you want to treat your body well, you've got to like it, or at least stop wishing it were something other than it is.
- Losing weight is not as easy as exercising and eating a healthy diet. Your mental thoughts, emotional state, spiritual lessons, and even planetary cycles can come into play.
- You look the way you do for a purpose: to experience what you need to experience.
- If you want to get a makeover, do it with the right attitude and for the right reasons:

  - Don't do it to match someone else's definition of beauty.
  - If you don't like yourself, whatever you do will be wasted.
  - Accept that you will always look like you, regardless of the changes you make.
  - Don't expect a makeover to get you what you want; it may simply give you confidence.

- To make a lasting change, you must make a corresponding change in how you see yourself.

  - Change what you say to yourself. Self-talk is subtle, yet profound.
  - If you are going to make comparisons, be realistic about it: compare yourself to people in the supermarket, not to celebrities in magazines and on television.
  - The longing to be beautiful is a longing to be free from shame. Open up with someone you trust and share how you really feel about how you look. It won't change your looks, but you'll feel much freer.

- People are experiencing a new kind of stress: the need to find purpose, balance, and happiness.
- Current planetary cycles are prompting us to wake up to our lives in a new way.
- Contact between Pluto and Uranus extending from the present through 2016 will help you wipe away the old and bring in the new by breaking down structures that are no longer serving you.
- Other physical symptoms of awakening consciousness are:

- Changing sleep patterns, especially the triad sleep pattern of waking up every few hours.
- Vivid dreams that feel more "real" than ever.
- Gaining or losing weight based on emotional processing.
- A more youthful appearance caused by positive changes in personal perspective.
- "Unexplainable" physical ailments that may be an expression of emotions due to suppressing what you really want to say or do. It's not just physical, anymore.
- New food sensitivities indicating that your resonance with certain foods is changing.
- Greater awareness of addictions and increased determination to eliminate them.

- Your physical body is the barometer by which you can measure your progress. It's not just physical, anymore.
- Appreciate your body for keeping your heart beating and giving your spirit a place to live.

TWELVE

USE YOUR GPS TO GUIDE YOU

Tune into your heart and follow its wisdom.

The GPS (Global Positioning System), is a revolutionary device that makes me think of the "evolutionary device" that is built into every human being: the intuition of the heart that is always there to help us plan our lives and find our way when we have wandered off course. Like a GPS, however, you need to learn how it works and then use it.

A helpful way to think about your internal GPS is to examine what athletes call "the zone," a state of supreme focus in which they are performing at their peak potential. When they are in the zone, they feel fully connected to the moment and consistently achieve their intended goal, which might be a basket or a certain score. While in the zone, an athlete's mind processes only the thoughts and images that help to execute a chosen task successfully.

Being in the zone during everyday life is based on the same principle. When we are present in our lives and in touch with ourselves in the way that is most inspiring to our being, we are happy and focused in the moment. We feel connected to a greater consciousness, and synchronicities and confirmations abound. When we are off-course or out of touch, we may be dissatisfied with life or feel unhappiness in our hearts that we can't trace the origin of.

Entering the Zone

To enter the zone, athletes know that they must be totally committed to their game plan. What's more, they must let go of doubts, fear of failure, lack of trust, and overthinking. The zone is a state of total involvement in the present moment without the mental burden of worry, doubt, or fear about results.

To be happy, you must be present with your life and live from your heart, which means being in tune with your spiritual self and committed to the game plan of your life. Like an athlete, you must constantly work to let go of your fears, doubts, and lack of trust. The first step is to commit to living life more from your heart. Your heart is your life's GPS.

Living from Your Heart

Living from your heart simply means being in touch with your inner self and intuition, and this arises out of being more present in your life. You may already practice being present to a certain degree, but as we grow and evolve, we must continually face the uncomfortable challenge of trusting what we feel within to take us to the next level.

The Present Moment

Getting more connected to the present is the key because the connection to your heart and intuition can only happen when you are present with your life. Mystics from times past to current day spiritual teachers have all told us we must put our full awareness on the *Now*, yet it is one of the hardest things to do because of all the distractions around us. However, it is not too late to start working towards a goal of being present, because everything from depression to frustration to experiencing a lack of creativity or feeling intuitively blocked is a result of *not* tapping into the resources of the present moment. When you focus on too many things at once and get distracted by all the voices "out there," you lose touch with the one clear voice within.

Intuition Is a Skill Not a Gift

Although it may seem that some people are intuitive and others are not, that is not true. The reality is that everyone is intuitive. Being intuitive and being able to stay in the present moment are skills, not gifts, as many think. The key to strengthening your intuition is to make a commitment to being more present. Your intuition is strongest when you are living in the present moment.

In addition, many think that someone who is "spiritual," practices meditation, and eats only organic, whole foods—for example—is more intuitive than someone who doesn't participate in these activities. The so-called spiritual person might just be stuck in the past, holding on to regrets and negative self-perceptions, and living in fear of the future—and not "in tune" with his or her inner voice, at all. While lifestyle can support intuition, it does not create it. The only thing that matters is whether your energy and focus are in the present time.

What are you doing to get present so you can hear your inner voice?

Cultivate Being Present

It is to your advantage to work towards getting present so that you can be more productive, feel more connected to a greater source, and dissipate fear and stress.

Following are some helpful ways to get into the habit of being present:

- **Reduce the number of things you juggle at one time.** Sure, multitasking can make you feel productive, but multitasking all the time creates scattered patterns in your energy field, and these are not conducive to being present. Concentration is a key to being in the Now, so practice using your attention to focus on one thing regularly. To avoid the typical distractions, use some of the tips, tools, and insights in Chapter Five to help you to focus on the day ahead.

- **Experience what you are doing.** How many times a day do you do something just to do it, without really *experiencing* it? An example is taking a quick shower just to get out of the house and make it to work on time versus *experiencing* the feel of the water and the moments of peace. Another example is eating quickly just to put something in your stomach versus really tasting the food that is nourishing your body. It doesn't take any more time to experience what you are doing; it just takes awareness and a commitment.

My Chinese uncle ate meal after meal with his eyes closed. I was a child, so I would giggle and make faces at him when he did it. In retrospect, however, I can appreciate that he was being present in the moment of an experience. At the dinner table, he often told all of us children to close our eyes so that we could "experience" eating. He told us to visualize the ocean when we tasted the saltiness in food and visualize the fruit on the tree when we tasted the sweetness of freshly-cut fruit. He told us that each grain of rice took months to grow and reminded us to appreciate the nourishment it gives. If you have never eaten with your eyes closed—try it! It is an instant way to become present with the moment.

- **Let go of resistance.** Anytime you feel stuck or find yourself in a situation or predicament you don't want to be in, relax. You can't get centered if you resist. When you resist, your mind races around, taking you out of the present. The next time something happens and you start to resist and react, catch yourself and refocus your energy toward feeling "okay" with it. So, if your boss says No to your requested vacation day or you can't find your keys or your car won't start, take a deep breath and start by accepting the situation. Even if you don't like it, acceptance is the first step toward getting centered. Only from the center can you gain insight into the matter.

- **Have goals, but let go of expectations.** Now, goals may seem like a contradiction when talking about the present because goals are based in the future. However, goals that inspire you are necessary, because they provide an overall direction that guides you in what you are doing today. Beware that your goals don't trap you in the future, which happens when the result (or your expectation of the result) becomes more important than the journey. Make sure to focus your actions, thoughts, and emotions in the present as you use your goals to guide you in the right direction.

- **Every day, appreciate what you have.** I can't stress this enough. Make it a habit to reflect on what you have and say thank you. It means looking for things to be happy about *Now* rather than later. Find reasons to be thankful for the opportunities that come your way as well as for the challenges.

When You Veer Off Course

It almost goes without saying that there will be times along the way when you realize that you are off-course. Wandering or even veering off course as you move toward your goal is unavoidable. When it happens, let it go! Easy to say and hard to do, I know, but even the most sophisticated and advanced jet plane ever built—the Concorde—constantly went off course.

Do you remember the Concorde? It was in operation for twenty-seven years, and it was an amazingly time-efficient means of traveling from New York to Europe. A commercial jet took eight hours to get to Paris, but the Concorde could make it in less than three-and-a-half hours. It flew too fast for human pilots to keep up with it: one miniscule wrong move would throw the jet off course, heading towards a different country. Because of this, two computers had to fly the jet. The computers would literally talk to each other.

One computerized pilot would say aloud, "We are off-track! Get back on course." The other computerized pilot would respond, "Recalculating. Correcting course." This would go on for the entire flight; if you happened to walk nearby, you could hear them jabbering: "Off-track!" "Correcting course." "Off-track!" "Correcting course."

I heard that a gentleman on a Concorde tour was curious as to why the two computers were constantly talking to each other. "Wasn't the Concorde ever on course?"

The tour guide said, "Yes, about one percent of the time. The other 99 percent of the time the jet veers off course and requires constant auto correction."

Autocorrect and Move On

It's natural in life to veer right, stray to the left, swerve up, sway down, and bump around. When the Concorde goes off course, no one gets upset. The computers don't scream at each other. They don't say things like, "You dummy! You are off-target—*again*!" They autocorrect and keep going toward their destination.

Since we all go off course from time to time, it would benefit us to follow the Concorde's example: autocorrect and move on. You may tell a lie that gets you in trouble, cheat and get caught, eat the whole gallon of ice cream and blow your diet, break a confidence, have one too many drinks, have a car accident because you were texting, lose your temper, betray your best friend—and so what? We all make mistakes, and we learn from them. It is part of being human. The important thing is to recognize what you have done, take responsibility, apologize if you need to, make amends, and then get back on course. So, treat yourself gently when you find you've gone off track.

What's more, if someone confronts you about why you did what you did, you can just say, "It seemed like a good idea at the time." At the moment of taking "wrong" action, a part of you thought it was a good idea. In that split-second, the benefits of taking the "wrong" action outweighed the challenges you would have to deal with later.

This is not an excuse for your actions, but it was the reality of your state at the time, and you made a choice that worked for you in that moment. Don't waste time or energy thinking that you should have been better or done better. Accept the facts and move on. The more connected you are to the present and to your intuition, the less frequently you will veer off course.

Use Your Intuition

Many people are out-of-practice when it comes to using their intuition. If this is you, start simply. The next time you have to make a choice—which restaurant to choose for lunch or what vacation package to book—instead of tediously weighing out the pros and cons in your mind as you would usually do, notice your physical response to each option. Close your eyes and put both hands on your stomach. Say one option out loud or think of it for five to ten seconds and note your body's response. Does it tense or relax? Notice your breath. Does it feel restricted or expanded? The best choice, of course, is the one that produces a relaxed and expansive response in the body.

Intuition and Synchronicities

The more you lead with your intuition, the more you will notice synchronicities. Synchronicities show up as affirmations to let you know you are on the right path. For example, let's say you are practicing leading with your intuition and choose to go to the Heart Café instead of the Logic Lounge for lunch with your friend. You made your choice because your expanded breathing and relaxed body response confirmed the Heart Café as a better choice. You know this means you will have to wait for a table and spend a bit more money, but you decide to trust this intuitive decision.

Before your experiment today, you would have chosen to go to the Logic Lounge because it is a time and money saver, however, while at The Heart Café this week, you run into an old friend who tells you about a job possibility that interests you. Note this as a synchronicity and affirm that you made the "right" choice. As you build up trust in your intuitive voice, you will hear it without the louder voice of reason drowning it out, and as a result, you will naturally start to lead with what feels right. Logic still has its place and its role, however, leading with your intuition will never steer you wrong.

Always Note Your Heart's Response

Make it a habit to note what your heart says in response to everything that happens in your life. Let's say a friend calls and asks you to lunch. Immediately, you feel that you don't want to go, but then you start talking yourself into it: it's been too long, you "owe" her lunch, she needs to talk, and so forth. Make the choice you are most comfortable with, but be aware of how you really feel. If you decide to go, acknowledge to yourself that you don't want to go, and don't judge how you feel as "right" or "wrong." Move towards doing what your heart says, knowing that in the bigger picture, this choice is the "right" one because it is heartfelt. If you choose to say No and feel bad about it, take time to list the potential benefits to your friend because you declined. This exercise will help to balance your perception.

It's Not All about the Brain

It's hard to lead with your intuition when you have been programmed that using your brain is the "smart" way to operate. I can understand this. I grew up in a bi-cultural environment where there was much opposition, but one thing my Chinese mother and American father agreed upon was the importance of teaching me to use my brain at all times. Anytime I acted spontaneously or made a decision based on a whim, I got a rap to my head and heard the phrase, "What are you, stupid? Use your brain!" It's amusing that some cultural phrases, when translated, emerge with a different nuance or confusion of meaning, however this phrase always meant literally the same thing whether I heard it in Chinese or in English.

In school, the emphasis was always on logic and reason, which were considered far more important than intuition and heart. In fact, I don't remember ever hearing any advice about them. No teacher said, "Follow your heart" or "Go with how you feel." It was all about intellectual reason, which is black and white and extremely limiting.

Glory to the Mental Body

Albert Einstein said, "The intuitive mind is a sacred gift and the rational mind is a faithful servant. We have created a society that honors the servant and has forgotten the gift."

Note the last sentence in the quote above. Our rational, intellectual mind gets way too much glory. When faced with a complex problem that requires a solution, we immediately engage our mental body and start weighing the pros and the cons to see what avenue of action is best. Understandably, we define "best" by the rules that we learned growing up.

We may weigh the consequences of what others will think, make sure that our choice minimizes the chance of failure, and of course, our final decision must minimize the risk of loss. The more important the decision, the more we try to find the "best" answer according to a rational perspective.

Use Your Brain and Your Heart

Did you know that our human brain's rational capacities are far more error-prone than our intuition? That's why the answer we think is "the best" may not be. The problem is, we are so afraid of making the "wrong" decision that we have a hard time trusting our intuitive instincts, so we usually suppress them in favor of logic. The reality is that complex problems you can't find a logical answer to are best solved by leading with your intuitive capacities.

I love the saying, "Your heart will never follow your mind, but your mind will eventually follow your heart." There is a lot of truth to it.

If you continually use logic to make decisions, you will keep moving further away from the essence of your heart. Your heart will never buy into what your mind tries to convince it of. If your heart is not into it, what you have to do feels extremely difficult and challenging. If your heart *is* into it, although at first you may feel a bit scared because your mind is trying to talk you out of it, stay with it and you will start feeling elements such as happiness, spontaneity, and joy. If you keep at it, eventually your mind will surrender its hold and jump on full-bore.

Bringing the essence of your heart into your decision making is a life-affirming practice. Even if some things don't make sense at first, your life will expand and grow in ways that previously would not have been possible.

Traits of the Happiest People

Only in recent years has the question of how to be happy been addressed through research. When happiness experts combined data, they discovered that all happy people have four traits in common. These are life perspectives that all the happiest people on earth share. Start practicing them, and you will be headed in the right direction.

The happiest people are on a search for themselves.

- The happiest people design their lives for joy.
- The happiest people avoid saying "if only."
- The happiest people *allow* themselves to be happy.

Remember Albert Einstein's words: "The intuitive mind is a sacred gift and the rational mind is a faithful servant." May you always remember to honor the sacred gift of the intuitive mind, use your rational mind as its faithful servant, and have the courage to live in your heart.

Key Points

- To be happy, it is necessary to be "in the zone" when it comes to your life, which means being connected to the moment and living from your heart.
- Getting more connected to the present is the key to connecting with your heart and intuition.
- Intuition is a skill, not a gift, and it can be developed.
- Helpful ways to connect to the present:

  - Reduce the number of things you juggle at one time.
  - *Experience* what you are doing.
  - Let go of resistance.

- – Keep goals in mind, but let go of expectations.
- – Every day, appreciate what you have.

- Sometimes you veer off course in pursuing a desired goal. When you do, simply autocorrect and move on. If someone asks why you went off course, a good response is, "It seemed like a good idea at the time."
- Practice honing your intuition by using your physical body's response to your choice of options.
- The more you lead with your intuition, the more synchronicities show up to affirm that you are on the right path.
- Make it a habit to note what your heart says in response to everything that happens in your life.
- Our brain's rational capacities are far more error-prone than our intuition.
- "Your heart will never follow your mind, but your mind eventually will follow your heart."
- Happiness experts say that happy people have four common traits:
- Happy people are on a search for themselves.

- – Happy people design their lives for joy.
- – Happy people avoid saying "if only."
- – Happy people *allow* themselves to be happy.

CLOSING

ENJOY YOUR JOURNEY

The goal in life is not to get to the end, but to find happiness along the way.

Ralph Waldo Emerson said, "Life is a journey, not a destination." Happiness, also, is a journey and not a destination that you literally arrive at "someday." Let your happiness be a state of consciousness that makes every day of your life journey expansive and meaningful. Happiness is found as you move through the key moments of your life with greater awareness.

Life Is Not About Always Being Happy

People often say to me, "I want to always be happy, like you." My response is that I am not happy all the time. Life is not about being happy in the form of feel-good emotions and constantly being upbeat and positive. It is natural for human beings to experience a wide range of emotions. If you hold on to the illusion that being on an emotional high all the time equals happiness, you set yourself up for a state of being that is impossible to achieve. Worse, that illusion creates unnecessary stress, which defeats the purpose.

So, even as you learn the skills to live a happier life and gain a more positive outlook, give yourself to permission to feel whatever emotions come up for you, no matter what they are. When you are feeling sad, remind yourself that it is okay to be sad. Letting go of the idea that you should put on a happy front all the time will not only reduce your stress, it will help you process your sad emotions naturally and restore your balance more easily.

Feel All Your Emotions

Happiness comes from knowing deep down that everything is in divine order, no matter what is going on in your life. Of course, things will happen that make you happy, such as reaching a goal, being productive, or seeing a cherished friend. As well, things will happen that make you sad. Either way, let go of the mindset that you have to be happy in order to feel good, and trust that everything that is happening has a greater purpose for you. During difficult times, remember that, in retrospect, whatever is happening will make more sense.

Happiness Takes Work

Use this book as a guide to understand your life better and navigate the obstacles that come up more adeptly. Use it to help you as you consistently strive to find a perspective that feels better. A state of happiness takes work and conscious effort; however, with practice, it becomes second nature. As well, you will be prepared for situations and circumstances that frustrate you.

Life Transitions

When professionals who counsel those who are in the process of leaving the planet compare notes, they find that people who are about to die have similar things to say. Dying people who had gone through the inevitable range of emotions—denial, fear, remorse, sadness, anger, and eventually acceptance—were asked, "What would you do differently if you were given another chance at your life?"

One of the top responses is in line with the theme of this book. They say, "I wish I had let myself be happier." Not until they saw the end of their lives did they realize that happiness was a choice they didn't allow themselves to make. When faced with mortality, they suddenly became wiser to living.

On their deathbeds, these people readily admitted that they had stayed stuck in old patterns and habits. In retrospect, they saw that it was fear of change that kept them pretending to others and even themselves that they were happy, when in reality they were not. They had longed to do things they wanted to do without worrying about what others thought. They had yearned to be authentic, live more fully, let go of rules, laugh, and be silly—and yet, they did not. This was their one regret. And here is an interesting finding: Facing imminent death, they all said that what others thought of them was the farthest thing from their mind.

Really Live Your Life

Choose to make each day of your life as happy, fun, and rewarding as you can. Living a happy life is just a matter of awareness, perspective, focus, desire, and having the right tools to get you there. Wouldn't it be wonderful to let go, be happy, and *really live your life* long before you are on your deathbed? That is the destination I wish to lead you towards: a state of authenticity, freedom, peace, inner joy, and of course—happiness!

ABOUT THE AUTHOR

Alice Inoue is a Life Guide who uses the modalities of astrology, feng shui, and spirituality in her work.

Born in San Francisco and raised in Taiwan, Alice attended the University of California, Santa Cruz, then spent four years in Japan before moving to Hawaii in 1989. She started out on a business path, but in an unexpected shift, transitioned into the world of media, first as host of a live, daily television show, then as a bilingual news anchor for many years, a spokesperson, and host of her own weekly Japanese television show.

Inspired by inner guidance and an awakening interest in spirituality, Alice made a bold shift and became an ordained minister in 2000. Soon after, she began intensive training in feng shui and astrology. She has developed a deep understanding of life cycles, timing, and environmental space dynamics, which she uses with her spiritual wisdom to help people understand their lives.

Alice makes frequent appearances on radio and television and has been prominently featured by all major publications in the State of Hawaii. She has a weekly column in the *Honolulu Star-Advertiser* Sunday paper, "Go Ask Alice," which offers insights into questions about feng shui.

Her first book, *A Loving Guide to These Shifting Times*, was published in 2008. *Be Happy! It's Your Choice* followed in 2009, *Feng Shui Your Life!* in 2010, and *Just Ask Alice!* in 2011, the last three winning Indie Excellence Book Awards. In 2012, she was invited to be a guest expert on Lifetime TV's popular morning show, *The Balancing Act*, featuring her book, *Be Happy! It's Your Choice.* In addition, she has produced three instructional DVDs covering popular aspects of feng shui in partnership with Oceanic Time Warner Cable.

Her company, Alice Inoue Life Guidance, LLC, is the venue through which she offers private sessions, public presentations, workshops, products, and more. She is the CIO (Chief Inspirational Officer) of her company and is inspired by helping others understand their life paths and awaken to their divine potential. Her goal is to help others lead extraordinary lives.

For further information and to sign up for Alice's newsletters and blog notifications, visit Alice's websites:

Company website: www.aliceinoue.com

Blog: www.aliceinspired.com

Made in the USA
Columbia, SC
22 December 2022

72585119R00080